Wayfare of a Soldier

A Memoir

MADHUR GOYAL

INDIA · SINGAPORE · MALAYSIA

Notion Press

No.8, 3rd Cross Street,
CIT Colony, Mylapore,
Chennai, Tamil Nadu – 600004

First Published by Notion Press 2020
Copyright © Madhur Goyal 2020
All Rights Reserved.

ISBN 978-1-63745-453-4

This book has been published with all efforts taken to make the material error-free after the consent of the author. However, the author and the publisher do not assume and hereby disclaim any liability to any party for any loss, damage, or disruption caused by errors or omissions, whether such errors or omissions result from negligence, accident, or any other cause.

While every effort has been made to avoid any mistake or omission, this publication is being sold on the condition and understanding that neither the author nor the publishers or printers would be liable in any manner to any person by reason of any mistake or omission in this publication or for any action taken or omitted to be taken or advice rendered or accepted on the basis of this work. For any defect in printing or binding the publishers will be liable only to replace the defective copy by another copy of this work then available.

I DEDICATE
MY DEBUT LITERARY VENTURE

In the loving memory of my "Dad",
Surendra Kumar Goyal (1928-2011).

"You are gone but your belief in me has made this journey possible. You were an avid reader and a great vernacular poet…… now I realize as to how I inherited this craft of prose and poetry".

and

In the loving memory of my "late wife",
Reena Goyal (1967-1999).

"You have left fingerprints of grace on our lives. You shan't be forgotten. I lived with your dreams and acted on them to ensure fulfillment. Hope you were a testimony to it wherever you are."

Contents

Acknowledgements	7
Prelude	9
Introduction	13
I. Gateway to Olive Green's: Indian Military Academy - My Alma Mater	21
II. Jat Balwan: My Extended Family, the Team Twenty	33
III. Happy Himalayan Kingdom: Bhutan	43
IV. The Kolkata Romance	55
V. From Mombasa to Ambasa	64
VI. The Land of Wind, Chill and Thrill: Ladhak / Siachin	74
VII. The Spiritual and Cultural Land of Sikhs: Amritsar	91
VIII. Tally Ho!! Armoured Corps: Bikaner	100
IX. The Land of Bihu: Assam	109
X. Sentinels of North East: The Assam Rifles	119
XI. The Tragedy: Bareilly	131
XII. The Cutting Edge: 34 Rashtriya Rifles	142
XIII. The Chandigarh Chapter	152
XIV. The Himalayan Land of Orchid & Kiwi: Arunachal Calling	163
XV. Shift in Ideology: Ncc Lifestyle	173
XVI. The Final Punch with Special Forces	193
XVII. The Twilight Years: Family Harmony	202

ACKNOWLEDGEMENTS

Writing a book is harder than I thought and more rewarding than I could have ever imagined............

Writing a book about the story of your life is a surreal process. None of this would have been possible without my best friend, **Col Nitin Chandra**. We trained together in the Indian Military Academy and were part of the same company. He stood by me during every struggle in writing the book. He would read all drafts of my chapters within minutes of sending them to him and would revert with his feedback. He boosted my morale and speed to finish writing it two months prior to my timeline. He is the one who wrote the "prelude" to my book. That is true friendship.

"I also thank my daughter **Ridhima Goyal** and her best friend **Saumya Ahuja** who are presently employed in Singapore. They both have been together right from college days and still living together sharing an apartment at Singapore. From reading early drafts to giving me advice on the cover to correcting my language so I could edit. Both of them were as important to this book getting done as I was. Thank you so much, my lovely girls."

To my sister, **Ruby Gupta** and brother-in-law, **Sudhir Gupta**: for always being the person I could turn to during those dark and desperate years. She sustained me in ways that I never knew that I needed. To my wife **Shikha**, my mother **Uma** and my son **Madhav** to be patient enough during those few months when I was not seen not heard and busy writing my book. Thank you all a big deal.

Acknowledgements

Very special thanks to ***"Twentieth Battalion the JAT Regiment"*** where I took birth as an Army officer and continued my journey into prosperity. I thank all my Commanding officers during my tenure and officers present in the unit therein for their all-out support.

My special thanks to ***34 Rashtrya Rifles***" battalion and all its officers served during my tenure for their true brotherly support in all operations we conducted together. The Gallantry award that I earned in 34 RR will always stay suffixed to my name thus keeping the unit close to my heart always and every time.

My thanks to ***"18 Assam Rifles"*** battalion that gave me the initial exposure to Jammu & Kashmir issue and the military way to tackle it. Sincere thanks to the Commanding officer and all officers serving during my tenure.

Special thanks to all ranks ***"1452 Pioneer unit"*** that I commanded and have very sweet memories about it.

My thanks to **86 UP Battalion NCC** at *Saharanpur*, **82 UP Battalion NCC** at *Muzaffarnagar* and **5 Rajasthan Girls Battalion NCC** at *Udaipur* with whom I have been closely associated with and got an opportunity to even Command them.

Thanks to the publishing house of **NOTION PRESS Media Pvt Ltd** along with my Publishing Consultant, **Saibhuvaneswari**, and Publishing Manager, **Mr. Anish Baskar,** for their continued support towards publishing and marketing of my debut venture.

PRELUDE

I recall the words of the author saying, ***"This autobiography has long been desired. It was initiated with an endeavor to record for the value of my progenies some information about their parentage or else the facts which would then go to the grave with me, leaving them with a hollow ancestral past***". Nonetheless, a dramatic shift came upon the design and it took on a life of its own to carry out self-recognition and self-realization. And, so what we have here is a complex amalgam of military musings over the past 37 years and pieced together with some storyline adhesive.

Military literature is packed with jottings of service officers on life as they saw it. Officers bloodied in battle, lead, perform and sometimes die, to bring victory and glory to their Regiment and the country. However, despite contrary orders, planning errors and paucity of logistics, victory is still achieved and remains a veil of secrecy.

This book is a first-hand account of a frontline combat soldier who led his men into glacial warfare and counter terrorist operations numerous times and as he says ***"there were abundant occasions when there was no reason for me to come out alive"***. Not only did he come out alive, he became a living legend on either side of Banihal Pass. The officer was suitably awarded for indomitable courage and conspicuous bravery with a ***"Sena Medal" for Gallantry***.

The book is in chronological order, spanning the career lifespan of the author. Each chapter deals with an important career milestone in the author's life. This book will delight the reader with its anecdotal content as well as huge amount of information (geographical, political and social) contained in each chapter.

This autobiographical account is by no means that of **Colonel Madhur Goyal, SM** alone. In fact, it mirrors the career life span of every single officer of the Indian Armed Forces because all have had an almost similar military journey. It is therefore a must read for youngsters who aspire to join the Defense Services, for all military spouses who would get an insight into what their husbands would have gone through. It would set many a young female heart aflutter to read about military life and look out for a future husband in military uniform. It would make excellent reading for brother officers in the services, for they too would be mentally teleported back in time and reminisce of their own times at the locales mentioned in the book.

The author has touched upon a very important aspect, not usually talked about by military authors, the emotional angle. Inside the battle hardened exterior of a soldier exist a heart which beats for his near and dear ones.... as a father, a husband, a son, a brother. Pangs of separation from the family, loss of a family member, jubilation on the children doing well, anticipation and joy of coming home on leave, are very beautifully elucidated in the book.

To a military man writing about tactics, warfare, fighting equipment comes easy, but to put it so lucidly wherein a person unrelated to the forces can easily comprehend, is what the author has been able to achieve. The author has studiously avoided the temptation to use archaic or terrorizing long words and instead opted for a language which is easily comprehendible to a large section of his readership.

This book is like a symphony, played by an orchestra. It has many players, of whom **Madhur** has been the protagonist. Contribution by the band of brothers has been drawn together and given a new shape to weave them into the book ***"Wayfare of a Soldier"***.

"A Batch mate"

(The band of 77' brethren)

Indian Military Academy

Introduction

Dawn of Time

"There is no greater agony than bearing an untold story inside you."

– Maya Angelou

Nowadays, there is no dearth of stories to tell. Artists, chefs, maids, porn stars, politicians, stand-up comics, spies, survivors of misfortunes—ranging from an unhappy childhood to cancer—are writing their memoirs. In this era of fake news, a memoir promises authenticity. More so if the subject is a Soldier from armed forces makes it all the more important. I, **Colonel Madhur Goyal**, the author as well as the protagonist of this story, have penned down exactly the kind of a memoir giving out my experiences lucidly of 37 rich years as an officer in the Indian Army including three years post retirement. Born in Oct 1963 into an engineer's middle class family, my childhood was spent in small towns initially. If you really want to hear about it, the first thing you'll probably want to know is where I was born, and what my lousy childhood was like, and how my parents were occupied before they had me, and all that David Copperfield kind of stuff, but I don't feel like going into it if you want to know the truth!!

My dad, **Surendra Kumar,** an intellect and an expert in his field was invited to a joint venture of United nations, Kenya Govt and

Introduction

Birlas for startup of a caustic chlorine plant in Pan African paper mills, Kenya entailing production of white paper out of pinewood. He was an alumnus of prestigious Banaras Hindu University for his degree in chemical engineering and a master's program in management. He holds the distinction of attending the international conference of chemistry at UN for two countries, India and Kenya. He was then on United Nations roster list as top 100 chemical engineers in the world. Dad has always been my hero and a guide in my life. He was the one I looked upon whenever I found myself in trouble. He was my guiding force for all the major decisions in life. In fact, I have never regretted adhering to his advice as it has always worked for me. My father was my role model for many reasons. First and foremost I admired his passion for work. Moreover, he was an austere personality, never fancied flamboyant stuff and lived an easy and peaceful life. An ardent reader and a great vernacular poet...... now I realize as to how I inherited this craft of prose and poetry. He passed away in 2011.

"Since God can't be present everywhere, He created a Mother". There is nothing that can come close to the love that a mother feels for her children. Women are inherently good mothers. A good upbringing makes the better future of a person and a mother does an excellent job to give the best future for her child. She converts a house into a home, because to keep managing household works and to fulfill all family members' requirement on time is no easy task at all. My mom, **Uma**, a highly read lady from an elite college of Delhi university and belonging to a highly reputed business family of Delhi, married my dad in 1959 and joined the mainstream as a simple middle class struggling salaried couple. She too has always been my idol in life as well as a great motivator till now, which would be reflected in the later chapters as we proceed ahead. Worked as a headmistress of a primary school (upgraded to high school later) in Kenya for 17 years, apart from her routine duties as a dedicated homemaker, truly a superwoman indeed!!

Introduction

It has been repeatedly told - Siblings are one of the best things our parents bring in our life. I am one of those few lucky ones who have had the best shares of everything God created. My sister, **Ruby**, has a special place in my heart and life till date. My sister possesses a strong character which you might read in motivation stories or in the books of stories of legends. We had a separated childhood though, since my dad was initially posted in Brijrajnagar, a remote industrial town of Odisha with inadequate worthwhile education facility and my parents were quite determined in providing her good convent education from the head start. She lived with our maternal grandparents in Delhi. We would meet often and she joined us subsequently for good when my dad switched over to a different industry in Kota, Rajasthan. The family lived in harmony for a few years with both of us studying in convent schools and enjoying every moment of it. In fact, she being almost four years elder to me was still my bestie and I never felt the need of other friends around me when she was there. Dad, due to his specialization skills was offered a foreign assignment in Kenya as stated earlier and once more the family got a jolt and parents had to take a difficult decision of separation from children for the sake of our education as the quality of education was substandard in Kenya. Self and sister, this time were stationed at our ancestral house in Saharanpur, Uttar Pradesh and our parents finally proceeded to Kenya in 1974. Sooner than later, when Ruby passed her higher secondary from Saharanpur, we had to shift once again to our maternal grandparents at Delhi for her higher education from a reputed college.

Both of us for the first time were lost in the hustle bustle of the city life, Delhi. Delhi has character. A rather strong character, that's elusive but all-encompassing. It is like the protagonist of a literary novel, leaving behind an entourage of unanswered questions for those reading it. Delhi, despite its two faces, has one heart. A heart that speaks out to you, making you listen sooner or later. To me, Delhi is a loud boisterous macho man who thinks from his heart but acts with his mind. And that's why it always seems earnest at first but eventually ends up disappointing you. Every single time it can't help it. Delhi, a city as old as time, but still with a teenage heart. My sis was studying in Lady Irwin College while I was in Naval Public school.

As time passed, Ruby's marriage got fixed to **Sudhir Gupta**, a well read and a self-made man who came from unpromising circumstances, who was not born into privilege and wealth, and yet by his own efforts, by pulling himself up by the bootstraps, managed to become a great success in life. Sudhir as a self-made man often had to overcome great obstacles to achieve his goals to attain success through education, hard work, and sheer willpower. On a lighter note, his marketing skills became so well known that he could even sell his company products to his chairperson unknowingly during chats. Since my parents were in Kenya, I could visit them once a year during my summer vacations and rest of the duration was spent under the care of sister and brother-in-law at Jodhpur. In fact I had begun to catch a glimpse of my parents in them due to their unconditional love and affection towards me.

Here I take a break from introducing the immediate characters of my memoirs before I joined the forces and became an entity. The other characters of my DNA waiting to emerge in the forefront are yet to be conceived. Years passed by, and I graduated with a Bachelors in Science degree in 1984 from the University of Jodhpur. Dad rather hoped his son would join engineering or medicine. However, 'What I was meant for was the army. All my life it had kept beckoning me.' It wasn't a bad choice. Aside from the adventurous life, the armed forces have always promised, the money then was good. 'I would be getting the highest starting salary there was in the country at that point of time.' At age 19 years plus, I joined prestigious **"Indian military Academy, Dehradun"**. The anecdotes from the IMA days will resonate with everyone who was ever a gentleman cadet. They read like 'Humour in Uniform': breezy, droll and ironical with a good punch line. However, they also offer insights into the military tradition, inherited from the colonial era that has transformed thousands of raw teenagers into disciplined, polished officers, confident and capable of leading men into combat. As a young officer in the Indian Army, you must develop and exhibit character—a combination of values and attributes that enables you to see what to do, decide to do it, and influence others to follow. You must be competent in the knowledge and skills required to do your job effectively, and you must take proper action to accomplish our mission based on what your character tells you is ethically right and appropriate. This philosophy of Be, Know, Do forms the foundation of all that will follow in your career as an officer and leader. The Be, Know, Do philosophy applies to all soldiers, no matter what Army branch, rank, background, or gender you hold.

In later chapters, the tone becomes more reflective. Commissioned into the **twentieth battalion of JAT Regiment** in Infantry, I saw action right from the beginning of my youngster days in tackling insurgency in North eastern states. Subsequently, in Siachin Glacier, the highest battle field on earth, Punjab terrorism and most importantly the high point of terrorist activity in Kashmir valley. Narrating a true action story isn't easy. What is told is, naturally, presented in the best light, the 20/20 vision of hindsight. What is unbearable, but sometimes equally heroic, is often never revealed. One has to strike a balance between what happened and what seemed to happen. This memoir succeeds in that by evoking the right sensory images. There is the inherent drama, but also the confusion, not just of the 'dust and smoke' of battle. I, Col Madhur Goyal was awarded **Sena Medal for Gallantry** for my indomitable courage conspicuous bravery in an anti-terrorist operation fought in Badgam district of Kashmir valley in Oct 2002.

Introduction

Life is a journey filled with lessons, hardships, heartaches, joys, celebrations and special moments that will ultimately lead us to our destination, our purpose in life. The road will not always be smooth; in fact, throughout our travels, we will encounter many challenges. Some of these challenges will test our courage, strengths, weaknesses, and faith. Along the way, we may stumble upon obstacles that will come between the paths that we are destined to take. In order to follow the right path, we must overcome these obstacles. Sometimes these obstacles are really blessings in disguise, only we don't realize that at the time. Along my journey I too was confronted with many situations, some were filled with joy, and some with heartache. How I react to what had faced determined the kind of outcome for the rest of my journey throughout my life. When things didn't always go my way, I had two choices in dealing with the situation. I focused on the fact that things didn't go how I had hoped they would and let life pass by, or two, I could make the best out of the situation and know that these are only temporary setbacks and find the lessons that are to be learned.

Time stops for no one, and if we allow ourselves to focus on the negative we might miss out on some really amazing things that life has to offer. We can't go back to the past, we can only take the lessons that we have learnt and the experiences that we have gained from it and move on. It is because of the heartaches, as well as the hardships, that in the end help to make us a stronger person. Memories are priceless treasures that we can cherish forever in our hearts. They also enable us to continue on with our journey for whatever life has in store for us. Sometimes all it takes is one special person to help us look inside ourselves and find a whole different person that we never knew existed. Our eyes are suddenly opened to a world we never knew existed- a world where time is so precious and moments never seem to last long enough. It is often said that what doesn't kill you will make you stronger. It all depends on how one defines the word

Introduction

"strong" It can have different meanings to different people. In this sense, "stronger" means looking back at the person you were and comparing it to the person you have become today. It also means looking deep into your soul and realizing that the person you are today couldn't exist if it weren't for the things that have happened in the past or for the people that you have met. Everything that happens in our life happens for a reason and sometimes that means we must face heartaches in order to experience joy.

Recalling the rollercoaster ride that Army life offered me. Right from the highs of operational success to the lows of losing friends and the pride mixed with stoic sadness, the helplessness of watching the bodies of colleagues being taken away in tricolor-wrapped coffins. Kargil War was indeed an emotionally numbing experience. My posting in Siachin and Kashmir Valley played an instrumental role in making the "who am I today". "There was no time to even shave. The beard grew. We had food at odd times." Did I starve? "Two-three days was no big deal. That was manageable". The routine at Siachin's post was a unique experience which will be enumerated in greater details in the chapter ahead. From a Lieutenant to a Major, the Military secretary's branch had issued my posting orders surpassing the number of years having spent in Army... I was certainly a widely travelled and a battle hardened soldier by now. While there is tremendous pride associated with working in the Army, there is a problem unique to the Army man that i was not spared either. I got married in 1990 to **Reena** coming from a polished household and daughter of a very senior railway officer, ironically, as if life imitated the art of films, I rejoined my unit with my newly wedded wife only to leave her at the single officers accommodation allotted to me while I proceeded to operational area where the unit was deployed in general area of Tarn taran, Punjab. Our meetings use to be generally on weekends if the commanding officer was kind enough or else on official leave days.

Introduction

It's true that a soldier is never off duty!! Sometimes the reality of our lives as a military family resembles a not so fun rollercoaster ride. Emotionally I feel like I'm a teenager in the midst of puberty, and physically I can't plan anything beyond today because things in my military life keep changing. Ah!! But such is the life of the Army wife too. And I know I'm not the only one. A roller coaster of mixed emotions is common during the deployment stage. The Soldier's departure creates a "hole," which can lead to feelings of numbness, sadness, being alone or abandonment. It is common to have difficulty sleeping and anxiety about coping. Worries about security issues may ensue, including: "What if there is a pay problem? Is the house safe? How will I manage if my child gets sick? What if the car breaks down?" For many, the deployment stage is an unpleasant, disorganizing experience. Don't hold grudges, don't be sad, have no regrets and don't even and ever try to spoil your life. No, never! You only get it once, make it worthy, make it special and yes life is worth living and whoever understood its worth will automatically start living a blissful life.

Lastly, I made an attempt to give you an overview of the book standing tall ahead to narrate a soldier's life through my memoirs wrapped up in its seventeen chapters and bring you as close possible to any soldier you see on streets tomorrow. My journey embarks in first chapter on fruition of my graduation from Faculty of Science, University of Jodhpur, Rajasthan.

Remember, on becoming soldiers we have not ceased to be citizens.

"I am a Soldier, I fight where I am told, and I win where I fight."

*– **General George S. Patton***

Chapter I

Gateway to Olive Green's: Indian Military Academy - My Alma Mater

It's time to say "adieu Jodhpur"!!!!

My mission graduation accomplished empowering me with a degree recognized globally. Additionally, in conjunction having cleared my "All India CDS (Combined Defense Services) exam held by UPSC" gave me freedom enough to stay calm and relaxed from running pillar to post looking for a corporate placement in near future. Therefore, the interim period of wait till I appear for my SSB (Service selection board) series of interview was planned to be spent with my sister at Delhi. My three years at Jodhpur made me fall in love with its forts and palaces, temples and havelis, culture and tradition, spices and fabrics, color and texture, a booming handicrafts industry, all add up to make this historic. Jodhpur also called the Gateway to Thar, as it is literally on the edge of the Thar Desert. It is also known as the Blue City, an apt name as most houses in the old city are shades of blue.

Summer of 1984 was on the verge to set in when I bid goodbye to Jodhpur chugging along in Jodhpur mail entire night and reached early morning at Delhi to be received with warmth by my loving sister, Ruby and Sudhir Jijaji (Brother-in-law) in their rented house at Greater Kailash, close to Savitri cinema. Sitting at the breakfast table and breaking my reverie, jiji (as I always addressed my sister) urged me to have one more "poorie" (Famous Indian bread that I relish). I declined and complimented on her beautiful house and got into discussion as to how do I plan to reach Allahabad for my SSB interview and procure all the kit items mentioned in the general instructions. I retired to my earmarked room, lay on the bed and heaved a sigh I had been holding for a while. I looked at the tall ceiling and reconnected to my schooldays at New Delhi, Rajdhani (capital), the City of Djinns, Hastinapur or Indraprastha (famous Indian cities during Mahabharata). Call it by any name or sobriquet you wish, but it's impossible to not end up remembering it by its most heartfelt, its unforgettable nickname "Dilli", with ample dil (heart) in it. Despite (or maybe because of) its vices, Dilli seems nothing less than a teaser. If you spend enough alone time with it, it bewitches you, making you fall in love with it like no other city. Soon, the relationship troubles start. See, even though Dilli loves, it is non-committal to the core. It is never sure about you, and you can never be sure about it either. It will make you feel terribly missed when you're away, but it won't care an ounce once you return. Like now I spent my good schooling years here, and now when I'm back, it makes me feel nothing. Not unwelcome, but not welcome either. It's as if I don't exist. It's a terrible feeling….. 'tsk tsk', it gives heartburns. The problem is you love more when you are loved less. You can't help but love this city for its indifference to you.

I was tired eating and chatting with jiji the entire day while jijaji was in the office. Enjoyed playing with my loving nephews, Uday and Udit. Retired early to bed as it was Sunday next day and we had dinner planned outside. The next few days passed away in harmony and preparing myself for my next journey to Allahabad. The day finally arrived and I woke up to the pitter patter of raindrops just outside my window. Thick drops descended from the heaven, splattered and trickled down the slope in tiny rivulets to marry the turbulent stream outside the house moving into the drain. It was a heavy downpour. By noon, the clouds had cleared and the sun shone warm and bright. I packed up for my journey by train and left my sister's abode for Allahabad.

It was a rather chilly early morning; a bunch of us looking not sure of ourselves arrived at the Allahabad Railway station. We received a warm reception by a team of uniformed men waiting to ferry us to the SSB Centre. My first exposure to uniformed environment where I found something common...... "Salutes whatever moves and paints whatever is stationary". We got into a barrack and after scrutiny of documents were allotted chest numbers. Hence forth that became our identity. I had not taken any formal training or coaching for SSB and just got into the grind of things as it came my way. On the day of our Individual obstacle test, where we were to clear 10 different obstacles within a span of one minute, and we were permitted to commence our test from either of the obstacle we wish to. I, being an awardee long jumper during my university athletic events, chose to start from it. As a matter of fact I took such a big leap that my left foot surpassed the dug in portion and landed in the hard ground whereas the right foot fell into the dug in area. I was in shear pain and it was either a fracture or a bad twist of ankle. In the heat of the moment I managed to crawl towards the second obstacle but in vain. I was picked up and taken in an ambulance to Military Hospital Allahabad. Fortunately, it was just a stress fracture and I escaped any plaster around my ankle but a crape bandage around it with a few pain killers. However, I was not permitted to go back to the SSB Centre but admitted at MH only. I thought that my dream was over to endure OGs (Olive Green uniform) with shining brass over my shoulders. I was still taken to the Centre in an ambulance vehicle daily to participate in all balance of tests. The final day of result approached and I was certain of rejection due to the above justification.

What happened later is all history!!!! It would be impossible to summarize it in a word or even a paragraph.

Joy. Ecstacy. Excitement. Delight. Tears.

The adjectives would run out before I am completely able to express the surge of emotions in that one second when my chest number appeared in the list of recommended candidates.

It was all there. There were big smiles on the faces of three more boys who made it. The people on the other end sat gloomy faced, teary eyed. It was indeed a mixture of emotions. When we returned to our barrack, I heard the NCO "Ustad" (Instructor) shouting to the civilian orderlies that…… "in char *sahib* logo ka saman rehne do aur baki *ladko* ka saman gadi mei dal do"(keep aside the luggage of these officers and load the luggage of the balance boys). What a shift in our identity in no time. We weren't even allowed to bid farewell to our friends who didn't make it through. I still had the doubt in my mind and during the tea party with the SSB president and staff; I asked in curiosity to the President…. "Sir, despite my accident during obstacle test and completing just one obstacle, still I am selected?? The SSB President replied straight forwardly, "*Son, we need officers not monkeys*". The words still resonate in my ears till now. Indian Military Academy, Dehradun had been my dream since I was in early teens and to see it turning into reality was really special to me. If you are really passionate about joining the defense forces, clearing the SSB would be one of the best feelings of your life irrespective of the number of attempts it takes.

"Remember, perseverance conquers all".

The doorbell rang!!

Ruby opened the door and was bamboozled to see me standing at the door with pain reflecting in my eyes and my left leg not actually resting on the ground. I came in and sat down, the entire conversation thereafter was a cloud burst of mixed feeling erupting from the pain in leg to the cheer in heart. The big question was that, my parents were yet not aware of these proceedings of clearing my UPSC CDS exam followed by SSB selection. We decided that we would just send a telegram to them and this is how it went……..

"Selected for IMA Dehradun, joining 16 Jul 1984". Leaving no scope for them to react and accept it as fait accompli. Dad was delighted with a chest full to display his friends however mom as a true emotional mother was apprehensive to send her only son into armed forces and blah!!blah!!

Finally the day arrived when I was all decked up to depart to Dehradun by train for my fresh innings to commence in OGs hereafter. I carried the famous Iron box, bedding and an airbag with my essentials. Dehradun express was the famous train ex Delhi which departs early morning and arrives at Dehradun by afternoon. A bunch of us looking not sure of ourselves arrived at the Dehradun Railway station. We received a warm reception by a team of smart uniformed men waiting to ferry us to the Academy located at the foothills of the Himalayas. It was a royal treat to be allotted a fully furnished cabin with all the material comforts well beyond a university student's imagination. And to top it all, we were also provided with the services of a trained civilian orderly to take care of our daily needs. Over a period of time these orderlies become inseparable part of a cadet's life during the entire training period developing mutual respect and affection. The one attached to me was visibly delighted when I told him the very first day not to wake me to serve the customary bed tea and biscuit. Instead, he should feel free to have them himself. This was by no means a generous gesture on my part, but meant only to provide me with an additional fifteen minutes or so of precious sleep. Soon, we found ourselves acquiring a new identity as 'GC' (Gentleman Cadet) with changed appearances, thanks to Academy barbers ruthlessly using their pair of scissors on our black and thick unruly hair famously called the *"katora cut"* (crew cut), which eventually becomes your identity to the world outside.

We were called GC as the academy expected its cadets to uphold the highest moral and ethical values. Inscribed in the oak paneling at the Eastern entrance of the iconic Chetwode Hall – a magnificent structure is the Academy's credo excerpted from the speech of Field Marshal Chetwode at the inauguration of the Academy in 1932.

Academy's credo:

"The safety, honour and welfare of your country come first, always and every time.

The honour, welfare and comfort of the men you command come next.

Your own ease, comfort and safety come last, always and every time."

In his inaugural address to us in the hallowed Chetwode Hall, Academy's Commandant, emphasised the significance of this credo in the army. Even though the GCs came from the diverse backgrounds with different habits and social and economic backgrounds, we were assured that the academy aimed at plying a vital role in remolding those differences and make the cadets into a homogenous group for the sake of instilling a common bonding, while at the same time, allowing us to retain our individual identity.

Soon we realized the Academy's role as a melting pot of diverse culture. Unity amidst diversity was on full display in the campus. We were, however, forewarned about the most grueling training schedules ahead aimed at nurturing our mental and physical potential with every GC being allowed equal space for growth within the given time frame. The pace of training at the academy was fast and grueling.

It becomes a test of one's mettle and physical capabilities and in psychological terms a foretaste of what the trainees would encounter in the battlefield, where there is no room or scope for explaining or rationalizing one's failure. The Commandant's address was highly motivating instilling a sense of pride of being a part of this academy with such a glorious past.

Transition from student's life to that of a gentlemen cadet living in a highly regimented environment with extremely exacting routine was not too difficult, though at times annoying with certain archaic practices thrust upon us. Early in the morning a first termer wakes up the entire company and hurries to start and finish off his daily routine, he's normally given a clearance time (0400-0430 Normally) after which he is not to be seen near the toilet. Second termer is given the privilege of waking up by 0430 hrs and thereafter freshens up and a third termer may use the bathroom whenever he wishes. He attends an early morning roll-call called the "muster fall-in" after which they proceed to attend their morning parade which can be PT/Drill. Morning parade is of 2 periods each of 40 mins duration. On some days swimming, horse-riding or BPET may also be done. I do not have to tell how grueling these 80 minutes are, but I've known GCs shed as much weight in the first period of the training. Soon, I realized that the army, as an organization, seemed loath to change. I moved as achieving my overriding concern was to successfully complete my training without getting distracted by trivia. The day would start with a rigorous Physical Training session, at the end of the session we looked forward to wholesome breakfast in the GC's mess with no restriction for the gluttons, as long as one scrupulously observed certain table manners including use of different kinds of forks and spoons as demonstrated at the beginning of the training. It was also a lesson that in the army, nothing is left to chance.

Being in the mess was a gastronomic delight. What followed thereafter during outdoor training, whether handling of weapons or negotiating obstacle course or climbing rugged mountains was more than adequate to burn all the extra calories consumed. As we moved on with the exciting training schedule, a very tragic incident took place within days of our joining the academy that even today it haunts me. During a BPET (battle procedure endurance test) 2 mile run, one of our ex NDA course mate just fell while entering the finish enclosure. He never came back to life thereafter. The entire course was hit and grieve stricken but we were told that in a battle field one does not pause to mourn the dead. Our mental toughening had begun in earnest. However, the next day, academy was closed as a mark of respect to the departed soul who was cremated with full military honors in the presence of his inconsolable parents.

Soon enough life was back to the normal. From the campus during clear nights we could see the glittering Mussoorie Lights, but we were not allowed to go out of academy's campus without first passing the drill test conducted by none other than Academy's flamboyant Adjutant himself, had endeared himself to all the GCs for his extremely charming demeanor. Once caught while returning after lights-off, I along with 3-4 GCs were marched into his office the following day for being awarded a suitable punishment for such horrific act of indiscipline. When asked to explain the reason for our returning late, we sheepishly told him that we had gone to watch a Bengali movie of Satyajit Ray (Bengali film director) which got over late and in our anxiety to return on time, we even skipped our dinner at Quality Restaurant, a favorite haunt for the GCs. The Adjutant seemed convinced. We were reprimanded with these words *"Don't ever you repeat this! And if at all, you turn up late for whatever reason, see to it that you are not caught"*. Thus our much dreaded *"summary trial"*, so to say, was over in next to no time. Needless to say, we got away lightly and never committed such *"horrific act of indiscipline"* again. I had an exposure of many visits to Kenya and my course mates were all aware of it. In addition I had a natural tan and somewhat thick and slight curl in my hair….. I was introduced to the *"drill ustads"* (drill instructors) as a *"Foreign GC"* (Gentleman cadet) and many a time I escaped the punishment.

But the most amazing aspect of training is reserved for the late hours of the night, when seniors ambush the defaulting juniors on one or more of umpteen rules in place and they makes sure that the juniors learn a lesson during *"fall-in"* (congregation of everyone). A GC is made to do unthinkable. Imagine gulping down water campers and then throwing it all out, thereafter imagine you being made to stand with your back weighed down with a load of 16 bricks inside your *"pitthoo"* (backpack) or going round and round in circles with your bicycle held above your head. Oh!! There are numerous other ways to screw one's happiness, its too long to even list out, front-roll, back-roll, side-roll, cream-roll, egg-roll, murga, patti parade, maharaja, all with a different meaning to GC. There are also punishments when one is made to do pushups or sit-ups all night long or made to climb up a rope and stay on top until told to come down. The most treacherous one was "Mussoorie nights" where in we had to stand in total attention with our swimming trunks on and face the Mussoorie lights and the cool breeze of Dehradun would take a swing with extra chill from river Tons and would just come up to us acting as a sword ripping us apart. No two days at the Academy are the same, although we people do not follow a strict routine, every day brings a new challenge, a new experience. In between GCs also get to stay and survive in the wild during week long camps, he learns to defecate in the open, skin a live chicken, light bon fires and mastering the basic battle skills. I recollect after the so called, Fxxk fall in, I woke up with my neck and shoulder absolutely frozen. It was impossible to proceed for any class and I had to report sick and visit the hospital. As per procedure, I had to take permission in writing from my Battalion Adjutant or else I would not be entertained at the hospital. When I reached the office, I requested permission to enter, but I was bombarded with a volley of questions as to why didn't I salute while requesting entry? I was in pain and gulped the wrath and politely said, "Sir, my shoulder arm is frozen". The Adjutant looked at me in anxiety now realizing the fun filled night of unofficial training I would have had with my seniors. He permitted me to report sick. Not to go further...... similar volley of questions showered on me at the hospital too.

Reminiscing my first term Novices boxing match, I was a beginner with no experience of boxing earlier. It was compulsory to participate and as luck would have it, the Boxing instructors made sure that the pair did not tie up to spare each other on getting hurt. In that case they would themselves get into the ring and ensure a good black and blue label on your face before you leave the arena. My opponent was GC Tripathi (Name changed), my weight class and a beginner too. The bell rung and for 30 secs we just kept rotating in circles and were summoned for the first time. Now, both of us were left with no options and started blasting off without even having touched but got knackered after round 1. When I got back to my corner at the bell for R1, I was thinking *"Hell I'm drained, how I am going to do two more rounds!!!"* Then R2 commenced and I planned to hit him at least once with a hard blow. I with my correct stance moved ahead like a true Sylvester Stallone of Rocky and as luck would have it, I got him on his right jaw. He punctured a blood vessel and blood oozed out. He was knocked out and I was declared winner. Although not too happy about it and lost my fight in the Quarter finals later. My second most amusing episode was at the horse riding club. I could ride reasonably ok, however, my best friend GC Singh (Name changed) was on a horse back for the first time. When he started to trot, he fell down on his face making the instructor approach him with annoyance and conveyed, *"You fell like a lump of shit"*. The GC said, *"Sir, I've never sat on a horse back before"*. To that the instructor replied, Ok try once more and this time he fell down even with more disgrace. Now the Instructor remarked, *"It's not your fault, it's the maker fault"*.

Despite having grown in a non-military environment, I could clear all tests, whether weapons, obstacle course, long marches with heavy loads, endurance tests, firings etc. with ease. But it was with some trepidation when we were asked to throw live High Explosive pineapple shaped hand grenades (36 HE) for the first time. Till then we had practiced throwing only dummy ones. These grenades were designed to disperse lethal fragments on detonation. Once the safety pin is pulled out and the safety lever freed, the grenade explodes in 4-5 seconds. Once the safety pin is removed the grenade must be thrown immediately, otherwise the grenade could explode in one's hand killing all those within a radius of 9 yards. An NCO instructor standing next to each GC helps them to ensure that no untoward incident takes place. Having thrown the first one to the required distance, I was more than confident while throwing the second one. I felt reassured when the Group DS watching from behind remarked "well done". I felt relieved that I had cleared the test.

In the GCs outlook there is always a lurking fear of not reaching the benchmark for each activity. Failure to reach the required standards results in those GCs being relegated which meant extending the training period. It was common for quite a number of GCs being so relegated. Those likely to be relegated were put on notice first. Even worse was the case of those who were found falling much short of the minimum requirements. They were sent back home. Under no circumstances, the training standards were to be compromised. With bated breath, we all waited for the academy to announce the names of those found fit for being commissioned. Much to my relief, I found myself as one safe amongst others. Quite a number of GCs were relegated. As the date of Passing Out was approaching we were put through rigorous sessions of arms-drill on the drill squire under the watchful eyes of Academy Adjutant moving across the Drill Squire seated on his well-groomed horse. It is a day that each GC excitedly looks forward to. So did I. Finally on 14 December 1985 our batch (77 Regular) passed out taking final steps together with those from NDA (67 Batch). Since my parents were abroad and due to commitments could not attend my passing out parade. However, there absence was fulfilled by my uncle, aunt and my closest of all my sister and brother-in-law along with my nephews. I was assigned **"Twentieth Battalion of the JAT Regiment"**. At the stroke of the midnight, after a brief piping ceremony, I along with others became a 2nd Lieutenant in the Indian Army — a proud moment for all of us.

Now it was time to look forward to the next phase of my army life at the JAT Regimental Centre for an attachment of 14 days prior to my departure to allotted unit. Next day, we all left IMA with a sense of nostalgia.

Chapter II

Jat Balwan: My Extended Family, the Team Twenty

The sabbatical of 21 days granted by the army authorities after commissioning furnished me a feel of a social animal once again that I had lost for the past 18 months. I met all my friends and relatives during this break and most importantly, had even gone for a short pilgrimage thanking God almighty for my successful and safe return. The night prior to my departure was flooded with yearnings of IMA days embracing two different worlds under the same roof...... fun and frolic with course mates and the drill "Ustad's"(instructors) watchful eyes making me still tremble in sleep.

I prepared for my next journey to Bareilly, the Headquarters of the JAT Regiment of infantry Corps. All newly commissioned officers from IMA joining Infantry (also known as the queen of the battle) had to undergo 14 days attachment with their parent regiment at the Regimental Centre. We were eight 2nd lieutenants joining different battalions of Jat regiment arrived at Bareilly, a city in the northern Indian state of Uttar Pradesh, located near River Ramganga. The city is also known by the name NathNagri (known for the four Shiva temples located in four corners of the region – DhopeshwarNath, MadniNath, AlakhaNath and TrivatiNath), Bareilly Sharif (AlaHazrat, ShahSharafat Miyan and KhankaheNiyazia (derived the famous Muslim Mausoleum), Zari nagari and historically as

Sanjashya (where the Buddha descended from Tushita to earth). The city is a center of furniture manufacturing and trade in cotton, cereal and sugar. The city is also known as Bans-Bareilly. Although Bareilly is a production center for cane (bans) furniture, "Bans Bareilly" is not derived from the bans market; it is named after two princes: Bansaldev and Baraldev, sons of Jagat Singh Katehriya, who founded the city in 1537.

All of us reported to the Adjutant, JRC (Jat Regimental Centre). After the initial documentation, we were guided to our guest rooms earmarked in the Officers mess where we would be accommodated for next 14 days. Once we were left free for the day, at the first instance we communicated through our natural instinct and dashed to the mess Bar and contemplated to polish off a few beers before we go to lunch. The rule book says, till you are dined-in the mess officially, you are not charged for anything you consume prior to it. So be it, and the fresh single star heroes learnt to play with rules from day one. As customary, the same evening we were to be dined-in the Officers mess and the Centre Commandant would officially welcome us.

As we say, one swallow doesn't make a summer; our fun filled environment got shattered with the arrival of the Adjutant at the mess. A tall, weird looking officer with a sadistic bent of mind shouted with a quiver of chosen adjectives at all of us saying, *"How dare you youngsters get into the Bar without being dined-in???? Just get lost.... and you guys are hereafter excused hard drinks (including beer) during your stay at JRC"*. However, we were invited for the party that night and seriously, it was the first and last time that we were offered drinks in the mess. It was so sad to spend more than double the amount and sneaking whiskey bottles from open market to our rooms in the dark.

Known for their valor and famous for their war cry *"Jat Balwan Jai Bhagwan"*, the Jat Regiment is part of the infantry of the Indian

Army, of which it is one of the longest-serving and most-decorated regiments. The regiment has won 19 battle honors between 1839 and 1947, and post-independence it has won five battle honors, eight Mahavir Chakra, eight Kirti Chakra, 32 Shaurya Chakras, 39 Vir Chakras and 170 Sena Medals…. Still counting. During its 200-year service history, the regiment has participated in various actions and operations in India and abroad, including the First and The Second World War. All of us had a busy curriculum for the entire two weeks enlightening ourselves with the history of Jat Regiment, daily morning 2 mile run and other BPET (Battle procedure endurance tests) in full uniform and kit with weapon, firing practices at the short and long range and troop games in the evening. Overall, the aim was to make us familiar with the Jat customs since we would be commanding Jat troops and this fraternity is undoubtedly too strong in muscle power as well as in high headedness.

Finally the day arrived and we were dined-out from JRC and boarded different trains to our respective units stationed at different locations all over the country. I was to join "Twentieth battalion the Jat Regiment", my allotted unit, and had to reach Hashimara, a small bordering town with Bhutan and Assam in west Bengal. It was a field station where no MES (Military engineering service) accommodation existed, in other words we had to live in temporary accommodation made out of self - help basis. The train went chugging entire night and the typical Bengali accent woke me up early morning. We had reached New Jalpaiguri (NJP), the famous confluence of Sikkim, Nepal and West Bengal. It is also the door step of the famous Siliguri corridor as we read in various military digests. The Siliguri Corridor, also known as the Chicken's Neck, is a narrow stretch of land of about 22 km width, located in the Indian state of West Bengal, that connects India's northeastern states to the rest of India, with the countries of Nepal and Bangladesh lying on either side of the corridor. The Kingdom of Bhutan lies on the northern side of the corridor. The Kingdom of Sikkim formerly lay on the southern side of the corridor, until its merger with India in 1975.

It was 5.00pm by the time train reached Hashimara, late by two hours. I got off the train and started to look for someone to receive me at the station but in vain. Sometimes later, I found one army *"jawan"* (soldier) with JAT written on his shoulder title and summoned him, introducing myself. He was overwhelmed with desire to meet the *"naya lieutenant sahib"*(new young officer) of the *"paltan"*(battalion). He called a few more of his colleagues around who assisted in picking up my stuff out of the railway station. Since there was no light vehicle available, so he politely said that *"a 3 ton vehicle is available here, if you could hop in, then we can leave or else the light vehicle would take another hour or so to reach"*. I chose to agree and we finally left. The fact that the effects of a sun set are seen earlier in the east and we were driving through a stretch of light woods as well as tea gardens, gave me a sense of pride as a green panther.

Before I go further, let me acquaint you with the basic structure of a military Unit. Army is organized hierarchically into progressively smaller units commanded by officers of progressive ranking. Smallest unit in an army is the Section, which contains 10 soldiers and is led by a *"Havaldar"* (Sergeant). A slightly larger unit is The Platoon, which consists of approx 40 soldiers but is usually led by a JCO. Three platoons, make up The Rifle Company, which has approx 150 soldiers and is commanded by a Major. Four or more companies make up The Battalion, which has approx 800 troops and is commanded by The Colonel. The battalion is the smallest unit to have a staff of officers (in charge of personnel, operations, intelligence, and logistics) to assist the Commanding officer. Several battalions form the brigade, which has 3,000 plus troops or more and is commanded by The Brigadier. (The term regiment can signify either a battalion or a brigade in different countries' armies.)

Now, back to my journey….. A prank is customary to be played on a 2nd lieutenant on joining the Battalion for the first time which was indeed fun. It was well past dusk, almost dark and I sat in the rear of the truck with all my worldly belongings that consisted of a steel trunk, a bedroll, and an army kit bag for things like boots, belt and other military equipment. It was almost getting dinner time when we arrived at the officers' mess. I got off here and the vehicle went off to the bachelors' quarters to off load my baggage where my batman (helping buddy) was detailed to set up my room. Soon after reaching the Mess I had to hand over keys of my trunk to be sent to my batman for him to open my box and prepare my uniform for the next day.

There were five other officers in the mess. They all welcomed me shaking my hand one by one starting with the senior most. The CO (Commanding Officer) was not there since he was out of station for an official meeting and I was scheduled to be interviewed by him the next day. I was offered a drink, which I refused politely saying that I did not drink (I said so after the bad incident at JRC, Bareilly). After our dinner, we as a group walked to our bachelor officers' quarters barrack. Before finally dispersing for the night to our rooms, the senior subaltern accompanied me to my room that I had not seen yet. My batman had almost finished setting up things in my room. He was ready to depart with my uniform to be worn the next day to work. He had to get it starched and ironed before next morning for me to wear. He had at least one hour's work before him on my clothes for the next day. Next morning he arrived in my room early with my uniform and the morning mug of tea. My uniform was stiff with starch and was crackling while getting into it. I reported to the Adjutant officially in his office even though I had met him last evening in the Mess. I was told that the CO will see me in a little while. I was to wait outside his office and go in when called. While I was waiting, the SM (Subedar Major) of the battalion showed up. He said, "*Ram Ram Sahab!! aapko Bees Jat join karne ki badhai*" (Sir, welcome to 20 Jat). He further said that he would take me for a round around the unit lines once I'm through with CO's interview.

Col NS Gill, our CO was a tall Sikh Officer on his second command to raise 20 Jat. He was highly experienced in all operations of war and the knowledge reflected from his eyes and every word he spoke. In those days for a 2nd lieutenant to meet the CO was not heard of. He was limited only to his Company Commander at Company level and Adjutant or maximum to Second-in-command at Battalion level. I smartly marched into my CO's office and was told to take a seat. He looked at me with a smile and asked me of my welfare and if I was comfortable last night. He explained to me the importance to be posted in a newly raised unit and more so being the first original commissioned officer of 20 Jat after the raising of unit. I could feel the pride and the adrenaline rush on his statement. My chest was full and the "josh"(courage) in me suddenly went so high as if I was ready to capture Islamabad all by myself. I was allotted 'C' Company (Rifle Company). This was a Dogra company since our unit was raised on a mixed fixed class composition comprising of Jats, Garhwalis, Dogras and Marathas. Once I was out of CO's office, SM was waiting for me and saluted me once again and took me along for *"unit darshan"*(unit familiarization). Later, I reported to my "C" Company commander in his office. He was a senior Major with adequate experience. It was amazing to be surrounded by officers who had lived through so much of battle experience for years and here I was who had only fired about 200 rounds(bullets) in my life at the Academy… from my 7.62 mm SLR/LMG and 9mm SMC/Pistol!! As days went by, I settled down in my unit.

It was January 1986, and we got the orders to move to our permanent KLP (Key Location Plan) at Binnaguri. The Cantt was a new construction with all amenities as per the modern age. It had a big club premises known as DSOI (Defence service officers institute),

Olympic size swimming pool, tennis and squash courts, a full 18 hole golf course with greens and the nineteenth was the Golf bar. A massive auditorium where movies were screened every weekend and lectures held by visiting dignitaries. I recollect a wonderful social evening organized on a Saturday at the DSOI, we were all enjoying the party when an announcement was made for couples to reach the dance floor for a competition and *"the best dancing couple"* would be awarded with a gift by the General. I was always ready with my dancing shoes, ironically was not married. Soon there was an announcement that it necessarily may not be a married couple and a friend couple is permitted to participate. I now became party to the offer and my known friend amongst the fraternity of *"Military nursing service"* was also present in the function. We started off and won the hearts and minds of the judges and crowd in no time and easily walked away with the first prize. I obviously handed it over to her who deserved it more to have partnered me. We had a beautiful Officers mess with separate condos' for each bachelor officer. The jawans were happy enough with clean and hygienic living area and new cook houses/ dining halls. Almost 20% of our troops even brought families to enjoy the life of a good peace station. The most important event in line keeping us on our toes was our *"first Raising Day of the battalion"* which was to be celebrated on 11 Feb 1986 in our officer's mess at Binnaguri. Although the battalion had nothing big to talk about in terms of war, serving in various terrain and training. However, the period was to establish a foothold administratively in conjunction with regular training in field of tactics, weapons and physical fitness.

The first raising day was celebrated with pomp and show with important rituals followed as, "Mandir function", "Sainik Sammelan", Lunch at JCO's Mess(Junior commissioned officers mess), "Pagal gymkhana cum chat mela", and finally the most enthralling of all was the big party at our Officers mess. The battalion left an impact on all invited guests as to how could such a young unit with barely one year of raising could manage such a magnificent function full of grandeur. It was not only at event management but at all competitions within the orbat of Headquarters 20 Mountain Division that the battalion excelled being second to none. We became the envy of all our neighboring units in no time. It's a matter of fact that a young Officer on roll of a Jat Battalion has no option but to be in the pink of health and supreme fitness at all times. Self and Hasmukh Patel my "senior subaltern" (immediate senior), both 2nd lieutenants were always found running cross country races, participating in various firing competitions or camping with the ITC (Individual training cycle) Company on the banks of a river. I enjoyed the ITC days the most where I was the only officer available in the camp with almost 80 jawans undergoing training at a stretch. I had my separate 180 pounder tent as my residence with a smaller 120 pounder at the rear as my washroom. The entire area was circumventing with a snake trench and the entrance portion had firefighting equipment as a safety measure. The early morning warm Sun rays would penetrate my tent through its nook and corner to wake me up and I would then take my boys for a 16 km cross country run. In fact I along with my unit cross country team was deliberately sent at the ITC location for practice in conjunction with ITC training capsule. Across the river were the foothills of Bhutan and I was very passionate about the area since I was aware that our paltan is earmarked to move to Bhutan very shortly as part of Indian Military training team to train the RBA(Royal Bhutan Army). I will elaborate on the trip to Highland Kingdom of Bhutan in my next chapter. I recollect one morning when I was training with my battalion MMG team (Medium machine gun), I noticed a jeep stopping by and our "D" Company Commander, Maj Kalyan Chakravarty dismounting along with a known person in civil clothing. I was spell bound to find my first cousin Nitin at this God forsaken place. Maj Chakravarty dropped him at my location, had lunch with me and left back to Binnaguri. It was indeed a surprise for me but I found Nitin getting swayed by the nature's beauty. He was mesmerized by the life I was leading in such mystic surroundings viz-a-viz what he experienced in capital city, Delhi. He had his fill of firing a Rifle, Carbine and even a Light machine gun. We took long walks at the river bank and finally had couple of tots of fauji XXX Rum and slept. He stayed with me for a couple of days and later departed back to Delhi.

Since I always had a passion for writing prose and poetry, I penned down a few verses in honor of my battalion on its first raising. However, as time passed, the poem kept on facing amendments in mentioning years of raising and more so that now 20 Jat is a pure Jat battalion with only Jat troops rather than the mixed fixed class one as earlier explained. The latest version of poem is as enumerated below……..

The Twentieth

"Eleventh February nineteen eighty five
The consecrated day of our life,
In the aura of immaculate garb
Engendered a salubrious infant,
A hybrid of four different castes
DOGRAS, MARATHS, GARHWALIS and the JATS!!
Professional strength and the courage so bold
Never lacked on any trophy's hold,
Undeterred by the desert heat or Siachin's cold
The valiant JATS progressively just rolled n rolled……
Now, thirty five years old, "TWENTY" …a strong mould
….Cuts like a diamond and shines like gold.

Reorganized to pure JATS but still an assorted cry
The cry for light and to learn the nature's life,
The go getter present and the mature past
Keeps the neighbor envious and the forces aghast.
The emerging fortitude and the expert tact,
It's not a fable, but an ulterior fact
All about the ardent" TWENTY JAT".

– Col Madhur Goyal, SM(Retd)

Chapter III

Happy Himalayan Kingdom: Bhutan

20 Jat, my paltan, had a role to play in Bhutan as per the training directive. Thereby, it necessitates terrain orientation and joint training with the *RBA* (Royal Bhutan Army) for better assimilation and results later. Consequent to orders for move, the entire fighting force was deeply associated in packing on war footing. I'll detach from the story line for time being and make an endeavor to relate the strategic significance of Bhutan to India in simple words.

Bhutan's significance to India stems from its geographic location. Bhutan shares 605 km out of total 1,075-km of its border with India. Nestled in the Himalayas, it is sandwiched between India and China. Thus, it serves as a buffer between the two Asian giants. Bhutan's value as a buffer soared after China annexed Tibet in 1951. As you may recollect the recent 2017 crisis in the Doklam region revealed that India will strongly oppose, even militarily, any Chinese attempt to assert control over Doklam. Securing Bhutan's present borders especially its western border is clearly important for India. Doklam in the hands of a hostile power would heighten the vulnerability of India's Siliguri Corridor, a narrow strip of land that links India to its Northeastern states. So vital is Doklam to India's defense that India has a permanent and sizeable military contingent and an army hospital in *"Haa"* district, where Doklam is located. Bhutan has economic value to India as well. It provides a market for Indian commodities and a destination for Indian investment. India also sees

Bhutan as a rich source of hydropower. A politically stable Bhutan is important to India. An unstable and restive Bhutan would not only jeopardize India's investments in that country but also provide a safe haven for anti-India activities and anti-India militant groups.

The areas of bilateral cooperation between India and Bhutan are diverse, ranging from economic relations and development assistance, trade and investment relations, social and cultural exchanges, all of which have paved the way for the strong ties between them. India has number of times wholly funded the five year plans of Bhutan, Indian defense services has contributed to training the Bhutanese army and the country has extensively taken the initiative of road construction in Bhutan through the project Dantak, under BRO (Border roads Organisation). India has also invested heavily in the major hydro power projects in Bhutan such as Chhukha project, the Tala project and others. On the international platform, India and Bhutan have been supportive of each other; India helped Bhutan with the UN membership in 1971. Bhutan has supported India on issues of the Comprehensive Nuclear-Test-Ban Treaty (CTBT), India's permanent seat in Security Council, etc. Besides, people-to-people interaction on formal and informal level has further enhanced their relationship.

Drawing back to the main story line, it was sometimes in Aug 1986 when the unit was all set to depart for *"Dukhey-Dzong"*, the west most portion of Bhutan bordering China and Nepal. We had around 50 vehicles (all types) for the transportation of manpower, arms and ammunition, complete logistics equipment, personal baggage and tentage since we would be camping at the earmarked site for a period of about three months. Adjutant was in charge of the lineup of all vehicles and consolidating the final report of manpower and stores whereas the Second in command was in charge of the convoy till we reach the destination. We also had a medico, Dr (Captain) SS Bakshi posted to us who would ensure good health to the battalion while at

Bhutan. I being the junior most officer in the battalion had the privilege of being the *IO* (Intelligence Officer) to the CO. I shared his Jonga with a map in my hand duly marked for navigation purpose. Finally the Convoy marched at 0700hrs after a comprehensive briefing by the second in command to all drivers, co drivers and all appointment holders. The likely time plan was to reach around 1800hrs with a lunch halt in between. The entire route was mountainous and not familiar therefore it warranted extra driving care to avoid any form of accident.

This was my first occasion to get so close to the CO and even got an opportunity to learn about him. He was a jolly person and in habit to ask a myriad of questions. Driving in COs Jonga and negotiating a bumpy ride across the voluptuous, curvy mountains was indeed a treat. He would invariably ask me the present location on map and I would start reading the map contours and correlating them on ground and finally about to reply when he would point out at a lake on ground and ask to plot it on the map. He would just look at me from the corner of his eyes and give a smile and then look ahead. As we moved ahead towards the watershed we could see the snowcapped peaks emerging from behind the clouds, to the view of which the CO and I went shutter crazy. As we started to descend into Paro valley, we could once again see the green grazing grounds, deep mountains, and the silver tinted course of Paro River. A huge billboard with the photo of the royal family welcomed us to the Kingdom. The clean air and the pristine beauty of the mountains suddenly made us super active and we halted our Jonga for a while on the road side and take a strenuous climb on the height close by from where we could take an aerial view of the balance of convoy following us. We were carrying our packed lunch and enjoyed munching "*aloo parathas with aam ka achar*"(Indian bread stuffed with mashed potatoes to eat with mango pickle). Soon we could sight the long trail of army vehicles approaching and while sipping hot mug of tea out of COs thermos flask, we decided to move further and reach the destination earlier so as to conform from the advance party on the arrangements made since they had already reached a couple of days prior.

All is well that ends well!! Entire movement was complete within stipulated time frame and the instant reaction of troops de-boarding the vehicles was to stretch them and take deep sigh of pure and clean air. It was a long day of travel and everyone had run out of steam. The unit Quarter master officer who had arrived with the advance party took control of the situation and guided everyone to respective areas where they would retire for the night. Hot food was served as a welcome gesture by the RBA. The Officers moved to the RBA Officers mess for a couple of quick shots of hot brandy to wear off the day's exhaustion and retired after dinner.

The first morning at Dukhye Dzong was a common reaction of all; I could see each one out of their habitat taking a 360 degree turn on their heels to acquaint themselves with the landscape around. This valley was an extension of Paro valley led us towards the end of the road leading to a huge fortified pillared gate which appears as remnants of a Dzong (Fort) thereby giving the name as Dukhye Dzong. It was a mesmerizing view early morning from the Dzong to witness the massive *"Mount Chomalhari"* conical snow clad peak literally giving a blinding effect to our eyes. The valley was surrounded by steep mountains, dense with evergreen forests, rhododendrons and bamboo, rural villages, the omnipresent monasteries, *"chortens"* (Lamaist monuments) and groves of colorful prayer flags fluttering on long poles, the wind carrying their appeals up to heaven. We soaked ourselves in the unhurried, unworried mood all around us. The Bhutanese love chilies. Their mouth-scorching meals and chilli-infused condiments can catch you by surprise. The local fare is likely to be the national dish, *"ema datshi"* (chilies and cheese), and meat of questionable vintage.

Two days of camp setting, food, revelry and hedonism flew off in a jiffy. It's time for serious work now — we got into our uniform and had a joint Sainik Sammelan (public address) presided by the CO while all Officers and Jawans of both Armies attended who were undergoing joint training. A well thought of training program was chalked out by the second in command who was also the training cum security officer for the event. Most of the Officers of RBA undergo initial commissioning training at NDA/ IMA in India hence they are well versed with the language, customs and drills followed by Indian army. They would rather act as interpreters to their jawans in case of any doubt. The first week was spent in area familiarization cum acclimatization process due to the average height of the area was over 9000 ft. We established a separate training arena for specialist Commando training with 2nd Lieut Hasmukh Patel as in charge, a short and a long range for firing of small arms, prepared squad posts for central lectures and smaller ones for weapon training etc. Our habitat was in snow arctic tent medium which was allotted single to a Major and above whereas, we Lieutenants and Captains shared two in one. We had an Officers mess too lodged in a large tent with a TV set and a VCR installed in it.

By the weekend, we were fully established and had commenced our routine training activities. The second week started and we had plans for LRPs (Long range patrols). Generally, two officers with two JCOs and 20 jawans would proceed on such a patrol with full equipment and rations to sustain for next 72 hrs or so. This was the best outdoor activity wherein I enjoyed the most. We always had a few boys of RBA and a local guide in each patrol. Tenzing, a shy and soft-spoken local, was our 'Raju Guide' for the trip. En route, he enthralled us with local nuggets and cultural trivia about Bhutan. Tenzing's equanimity in the face of our barrage of questions was our first taste of Buddhist detachment and composure. It contrasted sharply with our own beleaguered look due to strain and disposition.

Two days passed by in a jiffy taking pictures, marking maps and carrying out various tactical appreciations as task allotted. Some more food, merriment and pleasure-seeking and we were off for finally for the last leg of our LRP. Once we reached our base, the vehicles to the campsite arrived for our pickup. On termination of LRP, generally the next day is given as an administrative day for the Patrol party to recoup.

Coming weekend, the CO permitted all of us to take a day out at Paro town next door but we were supposed to be back by night. All Officers were highly thrilled of the breaking news and looked forward for an early morning departure. We got a modified one ton truck, and all of us sat down at the rear. It had cushioned seats, a floor mat, a music system and a water camper with a couple of glasses. We even carried a hamper with a few sandwiches and beer bottles. Not to forget favourite Tenzing, our Raju guide.

Paro's air is thin and pure, the sky a brilliant blue, and the surrounding mountains dotted with prayer flags — rather dramatic. We started our day by pledging a trek to Takshay Gompa (Now named as Tiger's Nest) but realized it was not a bright idea for a fauji on a holiday after covering barely one-third of the mule dung-dotted path. The Tiger's Nest is the mainstay of Bhutan attractions. It is believed that Guru Rinpoche arrived at this spot on the back of a tigress and meditated in a cave for three years, three months, three weeks, three days and three hours in the 8th century. The sacred spot houses a temple complex that appears precariously balanced atop a 900 m high cliff. Scuttling back to the base camp, we decide to shop at the roof-less stalls put up by the locals who seduce us saying, "*Sahab, thora shopping lelo... discount milega.*" Various items caught our fancy – Red shiny Bhutanese chillies, incense powders and herbs, handmade darts and knives. Trekking done with, we drive up to the Paro Dzong(also known as Rinchen Pung Dzong), a combination of monastery and district administrative centre, that resembles a medieval fortress in both, its construction and location. It was constructed in 1644 by Zhabdrung Ngawang Namgyal at the foundation of a monastery built by Guru Rinpoche. Walking across the bridge on the Paro River, we stopped to shoot a few pictures. The steep flight of stairs to reach the Paro Dzong tested our fitness once again. Entering the impressive central courtyard, we admired the colourful murals depicting Guru Rinpoche, the intricate wooden panels and a group of young monks immersed in studies (but occasionally breaking into a smile at the sight of two gawking tourists). We were there to have our sins expunged. A swarm of monks suddenly appears from the courtyard as we stumble over each other to get a picture with the ascetics. Then, just as suddenly, the flock dissolves in saffron blur at the far end of the dzong. Lunch at Uma, the purported Ritz of Bhutan, doesn't quite match up to the resort's classy ambiance, or its inflated bill.

We decided to stop by at the Jowo Temple of Kyichu, among the oldest temples in Bhutan. It was originally built in the 7th century by the Tibetan Emperor Songtsan Gampo. We were awed by the imposing idol of Guru Rinpoche as well as that of Buddha with eleven heads stacked up across five tiers. Interestingly, it is believed that the two orange trees in the courtyard bear fruit throughout the year. Well, the trees did have oranges hanging when we visited! We did save the best for the last! Just by evening at the Neksel Resort, Paro, was marked by champagne-popping and emotional bonding with our RBA colleagues who had invited us for a get together. Later realizing CO's instructions, we hastily packed up and got into the vehicle and managed to reach the camp site by 2200hrs.

The next week was spent in a major tactical exercise in a mountainous terrain. My "C" Company was in defense while "D" Company and one RBA Company were to carry out a deliberate attack on my defended locality. All the drills of such a scenario were performed including verbal orders by the Company Commander under supervision of Commanding Officer who appeared to be very judicious in his assessment. Various umpires were earmarked to manage the tactical battle at night also ensuring no accident takes place. The night of attack, I was very desperate and as a youngster had varied thoughts creeping in my mind as if it was a true attack and we were actually sitting in trenches with weapons and live ammunition. Just then I heard a war cry, *"Jat balwan, jai bhagwan......Bees Jat ki Jai"* I understood that the enemy has launched an attack and I started off with my rattler depicting the LMG(Light machine gun) fire and blasted a few No 90 training grenades to depict our action for defense. Finally, it was all over, and we were told to uproot from there and join up at the earmarked area for final de briefing of the tactical exercise. Initially the attacking and defending Company commanders gave their views followed by the Umpires who gave out the mistakes made by both the teams and finally the CO summed up the exercise and as always it was followed with chilled beer in the officer's mess and good food. We had a day off for administration next day.

As said earlier, we have an organization by the name of IMTRAT (Indian Military Training Team) at Bhutan. The Headquarters is at Thimpu whereas the major work force is located at Haa. We too got an opportunity to visit Haa. Once again we followed the similar routine of picking up our Officers one ton truck and started off for the journey of roughly 175 km (return trip). Instead of much-needed guardrails enroute, we found whimsical road signs — *'It's Not a Race or Rally, Stop and Enjoy the Haa Valley'*. And, every few miles, a simple, 'Thanks'. We reserved this day for a drive to the Haa Valley, about 70 km away from Paro and a top rated Bhutan tourist place. While an overnight stay at Haa was suggested by many guidebooks, we decided to return the same day given the paucity of time. We drove on winding hilly roads, past tall conifers and Buddhist temples. On reaching Chele La pass, the highest motor able pass in Bhutan, we stopped to have a cup of hot tea and admire the Himalayan vistas. At the Haa valley, we visited the Haa Dzong that now serves as the base for Indian Army as well as the Lhakhang Karpo temple. The visit was more official than a tourist attraction therefore I will not go deeper into it. After a quick meal with our Indian brother officers of IMTRAT, we headed back to campsite. Our spirits were lifted by the scenic drive and lilting Bhutanese pop being played on our music system in the truck.

Our trip to Bhutan was more than half complete and a few married Officers were given an opportunity to visit their families at Binnaguri while the bachelors got a free visit to the capital town, Thimphu. We journeyed along the largely empty road and we stopped en route and crossed the traditional suspension bridge leading to Tamchhog Lhakhang (temple) with impressive views through the chain-link bridge to the crystal clear waters of the Pa Chhu (river) below. Onwards to Thimphu on a road cut into the side of the mountain – for such a small country the immense scale and beauty of Bhutan is breathtaking: a sheer hillside rises to the right with the blue-green waters of the Pa Chhu to the left. Colourful prayer flags dot the landscape, the flashes of red, yellow, white, green and blue catching the eye as we drive by, cows lazily graze the roadside and see little reason to move and traditional rooftops are adorned with patches of red chillies drying in the sunshine. Children playing on the roadside offer a friendly wave as you pass by and giggle playfully as you return the gesture and locals dressed in the traditional *gho's* (for men) and *kira's* (for women) which at first sighting seem quaint quickly become routine.

Driving into the 'sprawling metropolis' that is Thimphu, population approx 100,000 of a total country population of roughly 750,000, I was struck by just how small a capital city it is. All buildings are built in traditional Bhutanese style with the main street leading towards the popular Clocktower Square – the city is a combination of the modern and traditional and offers a fun, if low key, night out and a chance to escape the hotel buffets. We learnt that Bhutan has never been colonised, perhaps a reason why its traditions and culture have been well protected and passed on across generations. The monarchy was established in 1907, with the coronation of the first Druk Gyalpo (King of Bhutan) – Gongsa Ugyen Wangchuck. We were also shown the living quarters of Je Khenpo – the spiritual leader of Bhutan who heads the central monastic body. We were worn out and retired in the royal guest rooms allotted to us under His Majesty's welcome. Next day our destination was the Changangkha temple, a Buddhist temple established in the 12th century. Huffing and puffing our way up the final flight of steps, we were rewarded with a beautiful sight: crisscrossed strings of Buddhist prayer flags fluttering in the nippy breeze, clouds wafting in and out of the valley below, arrays of prayer wheels whirling together in sync. We were not allowed to take the camera inside the sanctum sanctorum (the general rule in Bhutan is that if you are asked to take off your shoes before entering a temple, photography won't be allowed either). The idol of the Buddha at this temple is exquisitely crafted. Walking back to the Thimphu valley, a game of archery at the Changlimithang Archery Ground caught our attention. A group of spectators were cheering on two teams engaged in a duel. With our adventures in Thimphu over, we now drove back to our base campsite. The Joint training with RBA also came to an end and our plan to move back to Binnaguri commenced.

My trip to marvelously mountainous Bhutan will go down as one of my favorite trips to date. This small Himalayan gem has indeed intrigued me. We had one of the most unique travel experiences, exploring the ancient monasteries, fortresses (called Dzongs), ancient temples with prayer flags fluttering high, eating chilies and cheese, learning about Buddhism, and the immense warmth of its people. There are a lot of interesting and astounding facts about Bhutan, here are my top picks.......

- Land of the Thunder Dragon. The word "Bhutan" translates to "Land of the Thunder Dragon." It earned the nickname from the fierce thunder storms that often roll in from the Himalayas.

- Gross National Happiness. Bhutan is a country where development is measured by Gross National Happiness which is really amazing and inspiring. Rather than using the GDP as an economic index, Bhutan measures its overall "health" through the four pillars: sustainable development, environmental protection, cultural preservation, and good governance, which together form the Gross National Happiness or GNH.

- The Carbon-negative country. Bhutan is the first country in the world with specific constitutional obligations on its people to protect the environment and so it is the only country in the world that is Carbon-negative, that is, it produces less Carbon Dioxide than it absorbs. Among its requirements: at least two thirds of the country must be covered in forests and that figure stands at 72% today. No doubt the country is so lush and green.

- No need of Traffic Lights. There is no use of traffic lights throughout Bhutan. Thimphu is one of only two capitals in the world with no traffic lights (the other is Pyongyang, North Korea). There is only 1 traffic police booth in the main street of Thimphu. Bhutan is further trying to revolutionize the roads by encouraging the sale of electric cars.

- Buddhist democratic monarchy. Bhutan is a Buddhist democratic monarchy. Though Bhutan has a democratic constituency, the king of Bhutan — Jigme Khesar Namgyel Wangchuck and his wife Jetsun Pema are adored and considered as the topmost in the hierarchy across the country. The king has an open-door policy that allows any citizen to request a private meeting and share their problems.

- Consistency is the Key. You can see so much consistency across the whole country, in terms of their garment, architecture, branding, streets, name plates etc.

Reaching Binnaguri and settling in our rooms, we could hear the chirping of the birds and the whirring of the crickets. Overall an amazing experiences both professionally and personally as a paid holiday to say. My YO's (Young Officer's) course was overdue since the CO got it cancelled when I was earmarked to proceed prior to our induction into Bhutan. The course has three major divisions; Tactical leg, Weapons leg and the most infamous Commando leg. Most of my course mates had done away with the course earlier, however, my best pal, Austin Collaco, joined in this course and we had great fun. He was my Commando buddy too and I recollect hiding our cigarettes under our hat. Finally, I returned back with an "A" grading and having "Qualified" in Commando course was like an achievement of life (I vividly remember an American Lieutenant Clark, part of our commando course, having earlier qualified "Rangers course" in USA, and returned back stating this course is humanly impossible). Notwithstanding, I was back in the unit and packing our bags for our move to the city of Joy, Kolkatta.

Chapter IV

The Kolkata Romance

The battalion on reaching Binnaguri had a comfortable tenure for the next six months. We could recuperate our toes and heels from the blisters that occurred due to mountainous treks. The memories of Bhutan would refresh all by itself every morning on the lovely view of the Bhutan heights visible from our Officers quarters. Col Gill our CO had received his posting orders and the change of guard was to take place in our battalion. Col Pratap Singh was our new Tiger. he was tall, lanky, a totally hardened soldier but an ardent Bridge player too. It was difficult to believe that our battalion had eight officers playing bridge and every Saturday afternoon we had a beer and bridge session with two bridge tables placed to accommodate everyone. Leg pulling and sheer noise (on game getting over) as goes with the game culture of bridge was a treat to watch. A conversation during the game of bridge is still fresh in my mind. I recollect the CO and the second in command were partners when the second in command played a wrong card against the game plan of CO. The CO got so irritated that at the end of the game having lost the hand, he remarked, *"You can't handle 13 cards, how will you handle the entire battalion in war"*.

Relocation is part of Army life. One of the things you can count on is that at some point you will relocate to a different station, you may have to do it alone or with the entire unit. There is always a bit of excitement, anticipation and adventure each time your unit relocates to a new duty station. Sure you might miss the friends you've made, but each move offers an opportunity to see new places and make new friends. The unit once again received orders to move forthwith to Kolkatta for a short stint as the Garrison battalion in Fort Williams. There are two Fort Williams in Kolkatta. The original fort was built in the year 1696 by the British East India Company under the orders of Sir John Goldsborough which took a decade to complete. The permission was granted by Mughal Emperor Aurangzeb. Sir Charles Eyre started construction near the bank of the Hooghly River with the South-East Bastion and the adjacent walls. It was named after King William III in 1700. John Beard, Eyre's successor, added the North-East Bastion in 1701 and in 1702 started the construction of the Government House at the center of the fort. Construction ended in 1706. The original building had two stories and projecting wings. In 1756, the Nawab of Bengal, Siraj Ud Daulah, attacked the Fort, temporarily conquered the city, and changed its name to Alinagar. This led the British to build a new fort in the "Maidan".

Robert Clive started rebuilding the fort in 1758, after the Battle of Plassey (1757); construction was completed in 1781 at a cost of approximately two million pounds. The area around the Fort was cleared, and the Maidan became *"the Lungs of Kolkata"*. It stretches for around 3 km in the north–south direction and is around 1 km wide. The Old Fort was repaired and used as a customs house from 1766 onwards. Today, Fort William is the property of Indian Army. The headquarters of Eastern Command is based there, with provisions for accommodating 10,000 army personnel. The Army guards it heavily, and civilian entry is restricted. Much of Fort William is unchanged, but St Peter's Church, which used to serve as a chaplaincy Centre for the British citizens of Kolkata, is now a library for the troops of HQ Eastern Command. A war memorial has been created at the entrance of the fort, and the fort also houses a museum which displays artifacts from the Indo-Pakistani War of 1971, especially those related to the battles in the Eastern sector and the Bangladesh Liberation War.

The tasks of Garrison Battalion are mainly administrative in nature and at any point of time one infantry Battalion is always made available. We had to relieve the Gurkha battalion forthwith which was presently at Fort Williams, since they were moving out on operational reasons. Another major concern of urgent move was the ensuing 3rd SAF (South Asian Federation) Games to be held in Kolkatta for which an important task was allotted to our unit. "Twenty Jat", had by now mastered the art of packers and movers and in no time we were ready to depart from Binnaguri in Vehicles by road journey. The new location was a metropolis and The Fort William complex housed few of the top Generals of the Indian Army. The ambience within the fort complex was very formal and elite. Therefore, rather than our field uniforms, we had to get our ceremonial dresses for day to day activity including for the Officer Mess parties.

The season had shifted gears. The warmth of summers was retreating into the pleasantness of autumn. Flowers had seized the gardens. The move had commenced and I was eager to reach Kolkata, the city of joy, the city of culture and literature, the city of Gurudev Rabindranath Tagore, a Bengali polymath, a poet, a musician and an artist. In short, a creative genius! He reshaped Bengali literature and music, as well as Indian art and the first non-European to win the Nobel Prize in Literature. While entering the jurisdiction of Kolkatta, I could sense the warm smell of mustard and fish permeating my sinus. All arrangements in Kolkatta were perfect and our entire convoy of vehicles was guided into a posh and envied location of the city. The usual safety and security procedures of the unit were followed and the unit personnel were guided to their respective barracks. The CO presided over a quick conference with all officers in the Officers mess itself to pass relevant orders for next day and then we all retired to our guest rooms.

We had less reaction time for familiarization and were expected to gear up ab-initio for all our given tasks. The security setup was taken over at the outset along with other administrative duties within the Fort complex. There were two critical forthcoming events in offing at Fort Williams. Firstly, a major Eastern Command level War game was planned for which Gen Sundarji (The Chief of Army staff) and many more generals were to arrive. Lot of security standard operating procedures had to be chalked out in conjunction with the reception and accommodation of VIPs. Secondly, the 3rd SAF games were to be held from 20-27 Nov 1987 for which our Unit was given the task to manage the prize distribution ceremony on all days and events separately. It was the largest sporting event ever to be held in Kolkata, and West Bengal as a whole. This was also the first time when India hosted these Games. Apart from this, the unit had to give a "Guard of Honour" to the honorable President of India at the Airport since he was invited to inaugurate the Games open. First and foremost, as goes without saying in army was to ensure a good fauji haircut for all ranks and stitching of a new pair of uniform in same pattern and shade.

My *"achche din"* (happy days) were close enough as I was involved with the prize distribution ceremony event of SAF Games. Surprisingly so, I along with my senior subaltern (Lieutenant Hasmukh Patel) was tasked to select thirty beautiful girls in Kolkatta and train them for prize distribution ceremony. It was a jackpot for any Lieutenant of any Army of the world. I was the lucky one no doubt in the city of Joy. Now on a serious note, both of us planned out the entire selection procedure, gave advertisements in the vernacular as well as national dailies. We received a phenomenal response with manifold applications that we could ever handle. The interviews commenced and rightly following the policy of "rejection is the best form of selection", we finally honed on to fifty girls and subsequently selected final thirty with ten as reserve who would be on call if needed. Lieut Hasmukh Patel was also tasked for the Guard of Honour contingent therefore he had to stay away from the SAF Games training of girls for considerable duration against his wishes. A blessing in disguise to me indeed……. It was a unique task allotted wherein we taught the girls to walk straight with a tray in hand, ensured their visits to beauty salons for getting their face packs and hair done as per protocol, equipped them with Silk saris, traditional artificial jewelry and footwear giving a perfect Bengali look….. And not to forget a permanent smile was planted on their lips. My sister, Ruby, was present in Kolkatta then, since Sudhir Jijaji was posted with "Hindustan Paper Corporation Ltd" and they were residing at Salt Lake City just adjacent to the Salt Lake stadium which was the venue of 3rd SAF games. I use to occasionally visit her.

Hitting the bed and recalling my arduous day's schedule, on the other hand, Kolkata, I found to have an innate sleep cycle. Its residents sleep during the day, taking time off their vocations, shutting their stores, taking a bus back home for lunch, just to catch up on those two hours of siesta. I feel that's the true kind of satisfaction, of neither burning with unfulfilled dreams nor getting blinded by the comfort of being settled, but just being happy with whatever there is. For a Bengali, a cup of chai (tea) and a cigarette over a politically charged conversation could bring that joy. You are never short of thoughts and words while you are alone on bed and so was I and kept on penning down the important extracts to take a shape later………… It was 7.00 am and the soft doorbell woke me up from deep slumber. It was "*Chai*"; it's like a greeting to life. Every time you want to feel alive, you say "Chai". Chai is a living being. It breathes and eats. You would remember immersing a stack of biscuits in the chai, talking, forgetting about it and how chai gobbled it up in its deep recesses, never to be retrieved again. I remember how religiously my day began with chai and Parle G's (Biscuit brand) as a young lieutenant, so much so that now my teeth are the color of chai. We Indians are the colour of chai. All the Indian skin-tones are represented by the varieties of tea, from Assam tea to Darjeeling to Munnar tea leaves. Chai is the only beverage that is everywhere in India. The uses are deeply entrenched in our culture. When prospective in-laws come to see the bride, the patriarchal medium of introduction is chai served on a tray. If the bride and groom like each other, it's the tea that is used to deepen the colour mehndi that she'd put on her hands. It's the drink for the guests to turn into family-members, for friends to unwind and feel at home. For the family, it's a daily ritual—as frequent, if not more, than prayers. As I was paying my tribute to "Chai" I retired to my room, lay on the bed and heaved the sigh I had been holding for a while. Loneliness is akin to being swallowed by a swamp. You keep sinking deeper and deeper, and the weight above you only increases. You do not find a floor to gather yourself and stand up, to emerge. You let yourself be absorbed. This loneliness is worse than that of a beloved deserting you.

The journey from childhood to adulthood is perhaps the most important journey of every human's life. During this time, the events that take place, the atmosphere you're surrounded with, the books that you read & the friends you have, drastically shape the character. Some mature at home, without really moving out whereas most during their college or work — when the first streak of independence arrives.

The day finally arrived and our CO, Col Pratap Singh was all decked up to give Guard of honour to the honorable President of India at Dum Dum airport Kolkatta (then Calcutta). All is well that ends well, the inauguration was done with pomp and show and the direct telecast was witnessed on Television sets worldwide. As the evening passed, the confidence got more spirited and the discussions took rapid U turns. My sister had also seen the event and her first question to me……*"Who were all those girls surrounding you and Hasmukh Patel"*?? Any answer at that moment of time had no meaning or justification. We postponed the talk for day later. The situation wouldn't change and every evening hereafter she would be a compulsory audience during the 7.30 Pm Bengali news watching the similar scene till the event ended. Finally, she had to write a letter to our mom stating…. *"Your son is getting naughty on lines of becoming a flirt, better get him married soon"*. That's the day I got a gut feeling that I would find my bride from the city of joy, Kolkatta.

It is difficult to garner and pen down my thoughts about Calcutta. Too many memories, familiarity, and intimacy always jumble up my mind, so I decided to randomly mention the things I love most about the city. Kolkatta's street food is legendary for its taste and the city is a shopper's paradise. A walk down any of its lanes is an explosion of aroma, flavors, and textures. The city's homogeneous population and incredibly talented artisans (who flock here since it has a cheap living cost) make it one of the best places to buy really good handcrafted textiles, leather ware, and jewelry. Every nook and cranny of the city has at least one shop, boutique or street vendor selling beautiful hand embroidered garments or furnishings, painted ceramic products, hand beaded filigree jewelry etc. The city's street food, like shopping, is myriad and being blessed with an abundance of fish, vegetables, fruits, and tea, Calcutta street eateries consume all of them generously. Its British colonial history is also reflected in the street food and many interesting versions of proper English dishes can be found tossed up by the vendors busily. Chicken and lamb are consumed heartily along with generous amounts of pork. Proximity to North Eastern states and Nepal brings along a plethora of steamed, braised hilly delights, and momos (steamed dumplings) are one of Calcutta's favourite finger food. A huge vegetarian non-Bengali community gives rise to many mouth-watering vegetarian snacks, dishes and really awesome lassis (creamy yogurt drink). Come monsoon, and mangoes or the king of fruits appear like golden orbs and the much awaited silvery Hilsa (a highly flavourful indigenous Hooghly fish) thunder the markets creating ripples of excitement in Bengali households. The Vardaan Market (near Camac Street) kulfi vendors dish out creamy, deliciously cold, flavoured kulfis in fruit shells (orange flavour in orange hollows, mango in mango skin cups etc) by hundreds and the Hilsa fish festivals take the city by storm. Heart rules our heads in Calcutta and this is a city of readers. In Calcutta, befriend your local *phuchka* seller. *Phuchkas* or Gol gappas (as known in rest of India), are crunchy hollow dough balls filled with spicy potato, chickpea mix and served in sal leaf cups with a generous helping of tarty tamarind water. It is guaranteed to stun your senses, pucker your lips, and make your eyes water. Although nowadays, phuchkas are often served boringly tempered down or with curd, sweet water etc as per taste, a Bengali will any day swear by the original version. Vivekananda Park vendors are extremely popular and feature among the best phuchka sellers in the city. Such kind of adulation from a food-loving city is indeed a hard-earned reputation. The sunset is bewitching here and will captivate many hearts when viewed from a boat on the Ganges. Millennium Park, which is a pretty waterfront park is a must visit as many river cruises operate here. The starry nightlife makes it more interesting, as there are many clubs and pubs with good music. Kolkata is indeed a place for lovers.

I do not wish to end my Kolkatta romance here but the orders of olive greens specify "mission accomplished in Kolkatta" and we need to return back to Binnaguri. The Gurkhas (Gurkha battalion) had returned back and formal handing taking over of responsibility was carried out. We had to leave!! But I was to return to get my bride from here…….. Kolkata the second biggest city in India. A dazzling 350-year-old metropolis located on India's eastern coast, an artistic, cultural and intellectual marvel. The city has manifested a beautiful juxtaposition of the old colonial-era charm with the upcoming modern culture that grows amongst the city's young habitat. We finally reached Binnaguri with hoards of dreams to relish in the hours of distress.

Chapter V

From Mombasa to Ambasa

The emergence of "achche din' (happy days) were gifted to me by the city of joy, Kolkatta. As already highlighted, my parents were placed in Kenya since 1974 and I used to squander my summer holidays during school/college over there. Likewise after joining Army I still visited my folks for a big holiday on acquiring clearance from Directorate of Military intelligence during my 60 days annual leave. My leave dates for the year 1987 were approaching and all formalities and documentation was cleared by the unit staff for my visit to Kenya. Since our childhood days, we were four best friends combining our visit together to Kenya always during the summer vacation. Our dads were employed in the same industry at Kenya. However, now with varied jobs occupying our busy schedule thus did not materialize a timely get together here after. I was feeling uneasy travelling alone. My Air India flight departed from Mumbai to Nairobi with a stopover at Aden and Addis Ababa. Flying over Arabian Sea initially, then India Ocean, the aircraft entered the coastline of Aden and we started to descend but I was nonplussed since the airstrip was not in sight at all. It was worrisome till the airport complex was visible just at the edge of the rocky beach and we landed. It was very scenic and everyone appeared to be a sheikh to me dressed in "thwab"(traditional dress of UAE). Similarly at Addis Ababa, tall and heavy built guys didn't impress me much with a foul smell. Finally we landed at the famous Mzee Jomo Kenyatta international airport at Nairobi the capital city of Kenya. I saw my parents waving at me standing at the exit gate and a sudden release of Oxytocin from my brain connected the love and affectionate bond in depth and melted me all over. I just hugged my mom and dad with all love and I got rejuvenated instantly after hugging both of them since a long time. The thrill on our faces was noticeable and pleasing to all watching us.

Kenya, in East Africa is famed for its scenic landscapes and vast wildlife preserves. Its Indian Ocean coast provided historically important ports by which goods from Arabian and Asian traders have entered the continent for many centuries. Along that coast, which holds some of the finest beaches in Africa, are predominantly Muslim Swahili cities such as Mombasa, a historic Centre that has contributed much to the musical and culinary heritage of the country. Inland are populous highlands famed for both their tea plantations, an economic staple during the British colonial era, and their variety of animal species, including lions, elephants, cheetahs, rhinoceroses, and hippopotamuses. Kenya's western provinces, marked by lakes and rivers, are forested, while a small portion of the north is majorly desert. The country's diverse wildlife and panoramic geography draw large numbers of European and North American visitors, and tourism is an important contributor to Kenya's economy.

Nairobi, a sprawling capital city, like many other African metropolises, is a study in contrasts, with modern skyscrapers looking out over vast shantytowns in the distance. The lingua franca is *Swahili*. This multipurpose language, which evolved along the coast from elements of local Bantu languages, Arabic, Persian, Portuguese, Hindi, and English, is the language of local trade and is also used (along with English) as an official language in the Kenyan legislative body, the National Assembly, and the courts. Kenya is an undoubtedly gorgeous African country. Many dream of tropical weather, white sandy beaches and lazy afternoons out in the sun enjoying a cold beer and looking out into an amazing landscape. This is the very first aspect people consider when planning a vacation; the kind of weather their desired destination has? Kenya enjoys beautiful tropical weather with long sun filled days and gorgeous star lit nights and just enough rain to make a huge chunk of the country absolutely lush and just right for a gorgeous landscape portrait. I have personally witnessed all four seasons in one day literally.

Dad had a new possession, a Volkswagen "Beetle". The distance from airport to our Hurlingham flats was approx 40 Km and it was 7.30 pm by the time we exited the airport complex. Dad was expecting my demand to proceed to the famous *"Carnivore"* barbeque restrau which was enroute. The mouthwatering dishes were mindboggling and fully satiable. It has been everyone's favorite joint for a good meal (especially non-veg). We enjoyed tandoori chicken and seekh kababs while mom being a pure veg had baked potato with peas and soup. On reaching our guest house, we had a long chat discussing everything right from Ruby, Sudhir and both kids, all other relations, friends in India to the girls of Kolkatta as reported by my sister Ruby. It was a long day and we were all jaded. We hit the bed and woke up to an early morning cool zephyr. We had plans to leave for "Webuye", a small industrial township nestled in mountains within western province closer to the Ugandan border. We had to travel almost 500 Km, but distance doesn't matter in Kenya as long as one is driving through the Mustafas (Highways akin to autobahn's of Germany). Driving at 120Kmph is kid stuff there. The travel from Nairobi to Webuye is indeed mesmerizing. Let me explain so.........

First of all we witnessed the Great Rift Valley. Masai herders, herds of elephant, wide plains and dramatic escarpments all define the Great Rift Valley, which reaches through Kenya as part of a 6,000-km long scar that stretches from Jordan in the Middle East across Africa to Mozambique. Driving further we reached Lake Naivasha, home to Golden-winged Sunbirds, Superb Starlings and African Fish Eagles and subsequently Lake Nakuru with flamboyant crowds of pink flamingos whose massing makes for surreal photographs. The matchstick-legged birds could be seen feeding on the algae that give them their candy floss hue amid geysers that result from the lake's geothermal activity. We halted at "Nakuru" which is politically an important city. Our eating joints in all city and towns of Kenya are pre researched and chosen for providing a decent and genuine veg meal. Most of the Gujaratis (an Indian community) are running such joints.

Departing from Nakuru, we reached the highest point en route where the Equator passes through the heart of Kenya. Although it's an imaginary geographical line but generally all travellers halt for a while and get themselves photographed with the big Equator marked African map in background. We too clicked one. Ironically this point is considered to be the coldest place in Kenya. Moving ahead we arrived at the savannah grasslands. From the Masai Mara Plains to the Serengeti that straddle Kenya and Tanzania, the grasslands are simply breathtaking. But, we were not here to see the grass and spaced acacia trees, we were here to see the exotic wildlife that strives here. Zebras, gazelles, cheetahs, lions and a host of other wild animals indigenous to this part of the continent can all be found in these beautiful plains. The camera is always ready to go wild, literally. Just a few miles ahead, we were halted by a tower of Giraffes. It's a normal sight here. We waited for a while till they decided to let us go further. We reached "Eldoret" with a touch of a typical British colonial habitat. We halted for a cup of tea at my dad's friend's house. Dad has always been an ardent reader. He collected a few good books and a dozen of latest English and hindi movie video cassettes from his friend for me and we drove to our final destination Webuye which was just an hour away. Enjoying the scenic beauty, I saw a huge paper industry on the banks of a river, "Pan African paper Mills Ltd". This factory manufactures 350 tons of white paper per day and exports to 25 countries. The company is a joint concern of Birla Brothers (Indian Industrialist), Kenya Govt and United nations. My dad was the Chief engineer here. The entire habitat for employees was divided in three strata on the mountain feature which housed a captivating sight of a massive waterfall known as "Broderic falls". Towards the top of the feature were 21 independent bunglows for the senior officers and we stayed in one of them. Towards the middle contour was "60 quarters colony", for the middle rung officers and at the foot hill was "National housing complex" for the workers and other junior staff. We reached our residence and were warmly welcomed by our Indian friends and neighbours. Tired though, just crashed and slept.

There was a well kitted Institute for the officers with a swimming pool, an indoor badminton court, table tennis table, a well-equipped bar and a nice kitchen with dining hall. Playing a game of "Darts" was every one's favorite who so came over to the guest house. Arun, One of the group of my four friends as already discussed had arrived earlier and we were thereafter found moving together everywhere. Our plan of visiting Mombasa was chalked out prior to our reaching Kenya. However, we waited for a while to let our parents have a good cuddling session with their grown up sons and communicate the mental and emotional wellbeing with affection. Mom was the headmistress of a primary school and was busy during the first half of the day while dad would be back only in the evening. Arun and self would spend the day at the pool and playing darts or sipping a cold beer in the bar.

Finally the day came when we left Webuye on an 800 km long drive cum holiday to the east coast at Mombasa. Arun's dad was the General Manager, so we sneaked out his Citroen CX 2000 sedan. His dad also gave us the Company's driver "Micheal"..... In fact we asked for him since he had been with us in fun trips earlier too and was aware of our interests. He didn't even have a habit of sneaking to our parents of the secrets and was a teetotaler. We took a night halt at Nairobi and stayed at our company's guest room in Hurlingham flats. We visited the International Casino and tried our hand on Russian roulette, Black jack and Slot Machines too. Enjoyed scotch on the rocks and watched floor shows. We returned back to our guest room early morning and had to leave for Mombasa in a few hours now. Hurriedly we completed our morning chores and left Nairobi by 10.00Am. With lush plains, awe-inspiring mountain ranges, impossibly beautiful weather, a coastal region that rivals the Caribbean and gracious people to boot, Kenya simply blows your mind. The biggest passion for a youngster in Kenya is Rally driving. The Malboro safari Rally/The great east African safari rally of Kenya is very famous being a mud road rally extending to three days across the length and breadth of Kenya. Arun and Self had the privilege to be part of the service crew of a leading rally driver a couple years back. The only advantage for us was to drive on a tarmac unlike the rally drivers but the bigger disadvantage was to reach before they could reach so as to provide hassle free maintenance. Back to our route to Mombasa, Arun was driving the car now. It was a smooth sail ahead on a six lane elevated highway when I saw the "99 squad"(mobile police check point) a few hundred meters ahead of us. I shouted at Arun to slow down and he brought the car to a screeching halt just prior to the spikes spread out on the tarmac. The police officer moved in a dancing manner towards Arun and showed him the radar speed gun which read 164.5 kmph. He then asked Arun, "Please show me your pilot's license"? We were lost but found it amusing later….. Micheal, our chauffeur got down from the car and spoke to the officer in Swahili trying to resolve the issue. However, the officer was happy to state that, "I'm leaving you guys just because I got to test your brakes which work real well or else all the four tyres would have been in tatters today. Be careful next time and don't spoil your holiday in Mombasa."

We reached Mombasa and the beautiful Ivory gates of Mombasa welcomed us. Mombasa is the second largest city in Kenya, lying on the Indian Ocean and a host to the Coast Province administration. It has a major port and an international airport. The city is the Centre of the coastal tourism industry. The original Arabic name is Manbasa; in Swahili it is called *Kisiwa Cha Mvita* (or Mvita for short), which means "Island of War", due to the many changes in its ownership and the battles that brought about the changes in ownership. The town is also the headquarters of Mombasa District which, like most other districts in Kenya, is named after its chief town. The city is located on Mombasa Island, which is separated from the mainland by two creeks; Tudor Creek on the west and *Kilindini* Harbor on the south. The island is connected to the mainland to the north by the Nyali Bridge, to the south by the Likoni Ferry and to the west by the Makupa Causeway, alongside which runs the Uganda Railway. The port serves both Kenya and countries of the interior like Uganda, Rwanda, Burundi, Democratic Republic of Congo, etc linking them to the Ocean. Mombasa is one bestowed with such beautiful beaches with white sandy beaches and a deep historical and cultural heritage that most travelers cannot resist the beauty of the beaches and the history surrounding this city is simply marvelous. Just 16 km outside the city of Mombasa is the Shimba Hills national reserve; here one can see forest elephants, the endangered sable antelope Sykes monkeys etc and the Sheldrick waterfalls. Shimba hills national reserve is one of the last remnants of coastal tropical forests

The island life awaited our arrival in Mombasa. The Kenyan coast has a host of beautiful Indian Ocean islands that will not only take your breath away with the sheer beauty of the landscape, but with the kind of laid back lifestyle and weather found here. If you want to walk around bare-chested/topless, swim with the dolphins in the ocean and relish coconut filled drinks for days on end while taking in the beautiful coastal sunsets and enjoying the cool breeze that comes with them, then Mombasa and Lamu are the places to be. We had a booking in the Diani Beach Resort for four days of fun and frolic. In between we spent a day at Lamu Island. The only one word I can quote for that place in my memoir is *"**raunchy**"*. We went all the way to Malindi beach just to see the beach resort of the famous Indian filmstar Mumtaz who married business tycoon Mayur Wadhwani. Luckily, we could manage to view the couple busy with friends at the beach. We participated in various water sports….. went on glass bottom boats, tried snorkeling too. We had to buy coral sandals to walk on the coral reef. Overall it was a great holiday!!

We checked out from the resort and were on our way back when we decided to take a different route from Nairobi to Webuye, ie: via Kericho and Kisumu. On reaching Nairobi we had planned to visit the famous Nairobi National park which is easily one of Africa's greatest wildlife watching destinations, home as it is to the Big Five (African lion, African elephant, Cape buffalo, African leopard, and white/black rhinos). En route we saw the luxury tea gardens of Kericho and Tree Top Hotel. Its home to one of the Queen's favorite hotels. Founded in 1932, Treetops is Kenya's oldest safari lodge, and Princess Elizabeth was in residence here when she was told of the death of her father, King George VI, prompting her ascendency to the throne. "For the first time in the history of the world," wrote big-game hunter Jim Corbett in the Treetops logbook, "a young girl climbed into the tree as a princess and climbed down as a queen." Last but not the least; we had our final peek at the Lake Victoria in Kisumu before we returned to Webuye.

Weeks passed by making small errands but nothing to beat the most euphoric and justifiable cum memorable holiday at Mombasa.

Returning back to India was inevitable and with a heavy heart reached back to Binnaguri. I barely got the privilege of caressing my dreams and living in fantasy for a few days, the State of Tripura (farthermost north eastern state of India) was in news for all wrong things. Tripura National Volunteers (also Tribal National Volunteers or Tripura National Volunteer Force) was a Tripuri nationalist militant group had launched an armed struggle in the early 1980s to separate Tripura from India. TNV was led by Bijoy Kumar Hrangkhawl. As per directives from the Ministry of defense and our Army Headquarters, the unit had to immediately move and take positions in different hot bed areas of TNV activities prevailing. We had our battalion Headquarters at Ambasa with one Rifle company in near vicinity whereas the other three companies were spread out on different axis. The TNV was founded in 1978 with assistance from the Mizo National Front. It was initially called the Tribal National Volunteers.

A heavy pressure by the security forces in conjunction with serious talks at political leadership level led the TNV to surrender in 1988 and integrate themselves into a political party. The Tripura National Volunteers (TNV), through their letter dated 4 May, 1988, addressed to the Governor of Tripura and signed by Shri Bejoy Kumar Hrankhawl, stated that "keeping in view the Prime Minister Shri Rajiv Gandhi's policy of solution of problems through negotiations, TNV have decided to abjure violence, give up secessionist demand and to hold negotiations for a peaceful solution of all the problems of Tripura within the Constitution of India." The TNV also furnished its by-laws which conform to the laws in force. On this basis, a series of discussions were held with representatives of TNV.

The violence was over however the unit continued for another month at Ambasa maintaining area domination to make our presence felt and avoid any further misadventure by the TNVs.

Recalling my exotic holiday at **Mombasa** always made me dread the thatched hut I was dwelling in at **Amabasa** along with a swarm of blood hungry mosquitos always giving me company. We retuned back to Binnaguri only to plan for our permanent move hereafter from the Eastern sector to the thrilling Northern sector of Ladhak and Siachin Glacier.

Chapter VI

The Land of Wind, Chill and Thrill: Ladhak / Siachin

My Battalion was barely three years old but had gained tremendous proficiency in this short lap of our journey. We had matured enough to ask for more and we were immediately heard and assigned to move to Northern sector for HAA (High Altitude Area) tenure in Ladhak region of Jammu & Kashmir state. This time the move was by train and our Quarter master Officer demanded for the Rolling Stock (Military special train) for the move of complete unit from Binnaguri to BD Bari Rail Head near Jammu. I was all set to bid *"sayonara"* to my mushy memories of barely 3 years of North Eastern region.

Let me first apprise the readers with the concept of a military special train.......

Indian Railways and Army have an inseparable relationship. This special connection goes back to the creation of Indian Railways. One of the key reasons for establishing the railway network was to provide an efficient and dependable method of transporting large amount of troops from one part of the country to another, which enabled the government of the day to maintain control over the land it governed. Indian Railways operate Military Special trains all the time. These trains move in peace time and in times of conflict. Some of these trains are freighters only, while others have accommodation for personnel as well. Some of these specials carry men from the armed forces for non-military activities, such as earthquake or flood-relief work. Some Military Special trains have rakes formed totally by special "Military" coaches in their own distinctive green livery, while others have rakes formed by 'normal' IR coaches. Some movements get decided suddenly (for example due to natural or man-made disasters), while other movements are planned well in advance - as per the strategic relocations of operational units of Indian armed forces.

The rake, comprising of First Class and III class Military coaches as well as different types of freight cars was made available well in advance at Binnaguri Railway siding. Since we were moving to a non-family station in an operational area, the married Officers and other ranks were instructed to move their families to either separated family accommodation or opt to move to their choice stations/ hometown etc. In the week leading to the departure, everything was going to plan with the usual military precision. All the staff were excited about the departure, and were doing everything they could to assist one another. Finally, the day of departure arrived. It was Sep 1988.

A Military Special is an Operational Unit - on wheels. All 'ground rules' remain unchanged, with adjustments to suit the needs. The Unit Adjutant, who is the administrative head of a Unit, had his office in the one of the coupes of the 1st FC coach. The MI room (Medical room) was in another coupe of the same coach. This was manned during the day-hours by the Medical officer and personnel of the Unit. We even had an "Officers mess on wheels", as well as mobile cook houses for men to help with preparation of food items as needed en-route etc. The journey from Binnaguri to BD Bari took almost 3 days and was one of the longest, most beautiful and most tiring special train journeys ever experienced. The train cuts across the chest of India through the Indo-Gangetic plains, snaking through the tiny neck of a landmass at New Jalpaiguri that joins India. The train moved through the entire heart land of Bihar, UP and Punjab and entered the state of Jammu & Kashmir. There were no inordinately long halts, and the Railways handled the Special train very efficiently. At all stops, the train got admitted to regular platforms. All the stops for lunch and dinner preparation were at relatively major stations, where water filling was also done. After dinner halts, the train had long overnight runs. The actual movement between stations, as well as the halts, was well planned and coordinated. At each major halt, RP staff (guard) would communicate the departure time to the Unit Adjutant. The information would get passed down to every passenger via the staff in-charge for the coach. This information helped people to plan their activities, including bathing, washing clothes, grocery shopping etc. On arrival at BD Bari, the Military Special was received by our unit "advance party" who had already reached Jammu transit camp ahead of the special train.

It took almost one full day for unloading the military special and we had to establish piquet's to safeguard stores, material and manpower. Rest of the force was accommodated into the Transit camp close by and awaited release of heavy vehicles for our further move from Jammu to Srinagar and to Leh. I recollect an interesting incident at the railway siding..... There was a freight train loaded with cement from a private company which had arrived and was awaiting clearance from our special train to vacate the siding. The Cement train in charge, an employee of the cement company, appeared to be snobbish and was speaking rudely to our boys for clearing up soon. Maybe some of our *"Jat balwans"* made him bite the dust. That guy came running to the Station Masters office complaining that the Army guys are threatening him, saying that *"hum tumhe goli se maar denge"*(we will shoot you). He didn't realize that I and the Quarter master were sitting in the office. We heard what he said and looked at each other.....By then the Quarter master erupted in anger, *"Goli se maar denge?????* Humne toh bola tha ki tope se Udha denge"!! (Shoot you?????...... I remember having instructed them to blow you up with a howitzer). We could see the guy shivering and chewing his foot in the mouth. He mellowed down and with clasped hands requested, *"I'm extremely sorry sir, you can take your time to unload. I'll wait. Thank you"*!!

Jammu and Leh cities are places with unparalleled beauty. These places with panoramic landscapes are flocked with tourists from all corners of the world throughout the year. It is possible to reach Leh, one of the most spectacular places in the Himalayas, from Jammu, the winter capital of Jammu and Kashmir, through road. The total road distance between Jammu and Leh is about 741 KM and it takes about 15 – 16 hours to cover this distance. Our Army convoy takes a night halt at Srinagar and reaches Leh the next day. As per the Army protocol, we started our journey early morning with packed breakfast and lunch to have it en route. I recollect having crossed the Jammu Flyover leading towards Tawi Bridge. Once we were on the National highway, the convoy stopped and a break of 20 mins was given to eat our breakfast including *"bidi/ciggerate break"*. We continued thereafter crossing the military cants of Nagrota, Udhampur and the most cherished and scenic *"Patni Top"*, famous for honeymooning couples. We descended from the height and reached the Chenab valley to witness the ferocious flow of river Chenab. There is an Army transit camp functional at township of Ramban on the banks of river Chenab, the entire troops halted for lunch. Sipping a chilled beer and munching some peanuts on the banks of Chenab under the warm Sun and cool breeze brought back the human in me. There is an important fort known as Gajpat Fort, on the top of mountain. It is said that once Sheikh Abdullah was kept imprisoned in this fort for few days. In 1825, Gulab Singh had imprisoned Raja Sultan Khan of Bimbar in this fort. Sultan Khan died there and was buried at Chanderkote. In 1858 Mean Hathu Singh, the Governor of Rajouri and a close relative of Maharaja had revolted against State

Government and tried to kill Maharaja Ranbir Singh. Mean Hathu was arrested and shifted to Gajpat fort.

Post lunch, the Convoy kicked off for Srinagar witnessing the technological marvel of the BRO (Border Roads Organization) en route to Jawahar Tunnel also called Banihal Tunnel or Banihal Pass which is a road tunnel named after the first Prime Minister of India, Pandit Jawaharlal Nehru, it was constructed for round-the-year surface transport between 1954 and 1956. The length of tunnel is 2.85 km which facilitates round-the-year road connectivity between Srinagar and Jammu. It is guarded by military round the clock. A new higher capacity, all-weather tunnel (Banihal- Qazigund Road Tunnel) has been dug in May 2018 and is expected to reduce the traffic through the Jawahar tunnel when opened for traffic in early 2020-21.

When I crossed the Jawahar tunnel and came on to the other side overlooking Kashmir Valley, I was spell bound by the mystic nature and remembered the famous words of the great poet *"Amir Khusro"* defining Kashmir '**Gar firdaus bar roo-e zameen ast, hameen ast-o, hameen ast-o, hameen ast". (Agar swarg is prithvi par maujood hai, tho yahin hai, tho yahin hai, yahin hai)** or (If heaven exists on Earth anywhere, then it is here only, here only, here only).

The Battalion reached Srinagar transit camp by twilight and was instructed to halt here for next two days. We all retired to bed without much of a thought to wake up fresh to the chilly weather of Srinagar. I had the entire day available and along with unit officers paid a visit to the famous Dal Lake and the market to buy few warm clothing to guard us in the HAA of Ladhak. From Srinagar, Leh was about 450 Km, so by late evening we would be there. We crossed Sonamarg then the Zojila Pass on Pir Panjal range. The Famous "Drass military camp" was in vicinity adjacent to the highway and we stopped to have a cup of tea. This area is considered to be the second coldest inhabited place on Earth after Siberia. We moved ahead descending from the slopes of Kargil known as "Jalebi Morh" which as name suggests appear to be like "figure of 8" entire way down. We reached "Budh kharbu" from where the climb starts up further ahead to "Nimmu". Rivers Indus and Zanskar meet at Nimmu. Another 19 km of drive and we reached Leh Valley, a cold arid desert on the banks of river Indus. Set amidst the epic Himalayas, Ladakh is a rustic and heavenly beautiful travel destination. The rugged valleys and mountains, winding roads coupled with the vibrant cultural life maintain the exuberance and charm of this region. The iconic Magnetic Hill, the turquoise coloured Pangong Lake, the confluence of two mystical rivers, ancient and awe inspiring monasteries and the highest passes are a few of the marvelous attractions of Leh and Ladakh in general. At an altitude of 11600 ft, as we say, "Don't be a Gama in the land of Lama". It is essential to follow the correct acclimatization procedure. The entire manpower was adequately briefed of the procedure and small placards were made and displayed everywhere so as to remind us timely. It was a strict training to follow for next seven days so as to be considered fit for travel ahead to our final destination "Tangtse" which was approx 13000 ft. we were given Vitamin "B" (Red Colour) and Vitamin "C" (white colour) tabs after lunch daily. Our Jat troops used to call them "*Khoon ki goli*" (tablet for blood being Red in Colour) and "*Sans ki goli*" (Tablet for breath being white in colour).

We resumed our journey to our destination, a tea break at Karu military cantt and moved forward towards Changla (La means pass), it looked like a journey on top of white carpet and all the vehicles had to halt once again to fix the "*nonskid chains*" for further move ahead. Sun rays were falling at the far on Wari La top, making a serene experience. We moved forward, experienced a completely different view of Shakti Valley from top, the famous Z in the road and the chill in the air was getting heavier as we proceeded towards Changla. We finally reached there and what a look!! Changla normally has snow always on top but this was an amazing view, the whole world was white out in front of us and barring a few army personnel and few dogs there was no living being in sight. Amazing it was!! The down slope towards Durbuk commenced, the whole stretch of sand zones were covered by snow, we faced black ice on the road. Fortunately with nonskid chains we didn't have any accidents. It was amazing for me as my first experience to see how Army men fight with nature to survive in harsh conditions. We finally reached Tangtse to our permanent unit location for about six months till we acclimatize and familiarize well to get inducted in the actual battle in Siachin Glacier.

I was a Captain now with three stars on my shoulder. The CO, Col Pratap Singh appointed me as the Adjutant thereby keeping me into a spin hereafter. It's a very responsible appointment and forms the hub center or central control of the unit. In military communication codes, Adjutant is called a *"Lion"*. The Brigade Headquarters, our immediate senior formation was close by and my counterpart in the Brigade Headquarter was a Major holding the appointment of BM (Brigade Major). A BM of a brigade is also called *"Lion"* on radio code. Maximum orders, instructions, tactical and strategically important issues would be passed for action between these two appointments generally. It so happened many a times when we tried to speak, our call won't connect due to some disturbance or technical issue. The BM would feel that I was deliberately trying to avoid his calls when one fine day he along with the brigade commander was in our unit area for a visit. He light heartedly stated the recurring unhappy incident of call disturbance to which I promptly answered, *"Sir, when two lions roar at the same time, it creates ruckus in the entire jungle. Why blame the poor telephone set and cable"*?? The brigade Commander too was amused on hearing it. Although it was on a lighter note but the cable was changed and our communication setup was restored.

Our Battalion had an important role in Chushul valley, therefore regular visit to the area was in offing for area familiarization. Let me update you all with some significance of the area within limitations………The Chushul sub-sector lies south of Pangong Tso in eastern Ladakh. It comprises high, broken mountains and heights of Thatung, Black Top, Helmet Top, Gurung Hill, and Magger Hill besides passes such as Rezang La and Reqin La, the Spanggur Gap, and the Chushul valley. Situated at a height of over 13,000 feet close to the LAC, the Chushul Valley has a vital airstrip that played an important role even during the 1962 War with China. Chushul is one among the five Border Personnel Meeting points between the Indian Army and the People's Liberation Army of China. It enjoys tremendous strategic and tactical importance because of its location and terrain, which make it a Centre for logistics deployment. This sector has plains that are a couple of km wide, where mechanized forces, including tanks, can be deployed. Its airstrip and connectivity by road to Leh add to its operational advantages. Simply put, Chushul is the gateway to Leh. If China enters the Chushul, it can launch its operations for Leh. After the initial attacks, including on the Galwan valley by the Chinese in October 1962, the PLA troops prepared to attack Chushul airfield and the valley to get direct access to Leh. However, just before the attacks were launched, the area was reinforced by the 114 Brigade in November 1962, which also had under its command two troops of armour and some artillery.

An immediate challenge is of a flare-up, as troops of the two countries are deployed within a distance of 800 to 1,000 meters of each other. Logistics also pose a major challenge. There is a need to carry water and food to the top which soldiers cannot do. The harsh winter that lasts for eight months of the year poses a big challenge. It is very difficult to dig in and make shelters on the ridgeline. The temperature falls to minus 30 degrees Celsius, and there are frequent snowstorms. Notwithstanding all above, my battalion was completely in knowhow of things and in a commanding position to undertake any challenges what so ever. Apart from our training schedule, we spent time in playing games every evening and serious physical exercise in the morning. We lived in underground shelters with walls plastered with mud and enveloped with blankets to give an insulated feel. I had a fancy for drinking milk every morning which was my mom's dictate since childhood to drink at least a glass of milk every day. We were supplied with powder milk and I didn't like the taste a bit so I asked the village head if he could arrange to supply 250 ml of Yak milk to me on cash payment every morning. He was more than happy to oblige me and since that day, his daughter (I used to call her Dolma) would reach me at precisely 06.30 am every morning with milk. She would just make one sweet call and I would be off my bed in that bitter cold too. This situation made my helper (buddy/batman) very emotional. He stopped talking to me and one fine day I asked him the reason as to why is he so quiet these days? He hesitated but replied, "*Sahab ji (sir), I come with your cup of tea at 06.00 am and keep shouting but you won't wake up, however with just one call from Dolma you get up soon enough*". I got the message.... His ego was hurt and I ensured that hereafter Dolma would hand over the milk cup to my helper rather than get it inside. Smiles returned back on my buddy's face.

The severe winters of Chushul valley gave us good exposure and primed us up prior to our move to Siachin Glacier for which our unit was already earmarked to proceed in Aug 1989. As the day arrived, we were all set to roll backwards to Changla Pass – Bypass Leh - Khardungla Pass (the highest motor able road on earth) – Khalsar – Partapur – Painamik – Base camp for Central glacier. Before I go further, let me acquaint you with the importance of Siachin Glacier from our perspective as well as the adversary.

The Siachen glacier demarcates central Asia from the Indian subcontinent, and separates Pakistan from China in the region. The

Saltoro Ridge of the Siachin glacier serves as a divide that prevents direct linking of PoK (Pakistan Occupied Kashmir) with China, stopping them to develop geographical military linkages in the area. Siachen also serves as a watchtower for India to keep a deep watch on Gilgit and Baltistan regions of Pakistan. If Pakistan gets the location advantage in Siachen, it would become a big threat to India from the west in Ladakh in addition to Chinese threats from Aksai Chin in the east. Due to its control over Saltoro Ridge, India is better placed to strike a bargain while settling bilateral territorial disputes with Pakistan in future. Siachen also helps India to keep a close watch on China's activities as Beijing has vastly improved its infrastructure in this region. China has developed all weather rail and road links in the Shaksgam region, which was ceded to China by Pakistan in 1960s. Ceding Indian-controlled Karakoram Pass triangle region to Pakistan would have further strengthened the Sino-Pakistan footprints on these strategic heights. Besides the twin military threats from Pakistan and China, the climate condition is the biggest challenge for the armed forces.

Temperature in Siachen glacier in winters drops to below -60 degrees C. There are constant threats of avalanches, crevasses on the glacier, high-speed winds. Soldiers stationed in the area are affected by a range of fatal altitude related ailments like frost bites, hypoxia, hypothermia and white outs. Both India and Pakistan have deployed around 5,000 troops (brigade strength). In terms of human cost, as many as 900 Indian soldiers have lost their lives in Siachen since 1984 due to climatic conditions, in comparison to around 2000 Pakistani soldiers. In one of the worst-known incidents, 140 Pakistani soldiers were killed after an avalanche slammed into their army camp in Gyari region of Siachen in 2012. Pakistan was first to see the potential of this strategically-important unoccupied area. However it didn't deploy troops till 1970 but used to send mountaineering expeditions to the glaciers.

In early 1981, Indian Army Col Narinder Bull Kumar sounded the alarm over Pakistan's expeditions in the region. After that the army gave him the permission to map the entire region. Sensing Indian Army's interest in the region, Pakistan Army planned a mission to occupy the area but was hit by an intelligence failure. Pakistan had ordered mountaineering gears from a London company who was also a supplier for India. India got the information about Pakistan's acquisitions. In April 1984, India urgently dispatched troops to Siachen under secret *"Operation Meghdoot"*. Indian troops reached the glacier a week earlier than Pakistan. By the time Pakistan soldiers reached the region, India had already got control of the glacier and the adjacent Saltoro ridge, using Col Kumar's maps. One of the key Indian installations in Siachen is named "Kumar Base" after him. The glacier's melting waters are the main source of the Nubra River in the Indian region of Ladakh, which drains into the Shyok River. The Shyok in turn joins the 3000 kilometre-long Indus River which flows through Pakistan. Thus, the glacier is a major source of the Indus and feeds the largest irrigation system in the world.

Our induction commenced and we reached the base camp. Our Battalion took over Operational responsibility of Central glacier from 2nd Battalion the Dogra Regiment in Aug 1989. Initially the inducting unit had to undergo snow and avalanche training under the aegis of "Siachin Battle School" available at the base camp itself. We learnt the art of wearing Special Siachin clothing issued from the army ordnance detachment. Subsequently we learnt the art of wearing crampons to climb ice walls. Use of ice axe and pitons was also taught. Learning first aid to help the needy in subzero temperature was most important. Crossing a crevice site and assessment of avalanches and dealing with them if caught was also taught including use of rope Manila with carabineer. Overall within a span of three weeks our troops were confident enough to tackle this challenge and even marked fit to climb Mount Everest. The induction into the glacial terrain commenced and every morning at 04.00 am, as Adjutant, I would stand out and supervise departure of all parties to various posts. Every individual irrespective of any rank had to spend minimum 90 days at a post on glacier only then the reliever would be dispatched. Since I was performing the duties of Adjutant, my turn was in the second round.

The environment was loud and noisy the whole day with heavy artillery shelling by the Pakistanis and similarly the reply by our Bofors Guns. At times a sudden thunder of anti-aircraft gunfire would send shock waves in your body. The Battalion was very fortunate enough for not witnessing any war casualty during our tenure. Some interesting episodes kept on happening adding humour to the wind, chill and thrill. I recollect, once I was on High Frequency net and got hooked onto a personal conversation between a "Pakistani officer and his wife supposedly". I was hearing it for a while then I thought of entering into the conversation inviting some fun….. I interfered and started to call my friend and suddenly the lady on other side was taken aback saying, "hai Allah yeh kaun aagaya" and said Roger out. Similarly, our Company Commanders on the posts would ask for liquor which was strictly prohibited in view of the altitude and rarefied atmosphere, No post was below 18000 ft and ranging up to 22000 ft. I could not materialize their demands and would regularly face their wrath on phone/radio call. Thereafter they learnt the art of making codes with their respective link patrols to send them a bottle of brandy if they ask for a toothpaste and likewise. Once during lunch time, we were playing a game of bridge and sipping beer, a call from a Company Commander was received by me who just started to shout on me as to why didn't I send him "Times of India" newspaper. I told him that I did send him "Hindustan Times" instead but that did not satiate his need. He kept on shouting, ultimately I asked him as to what's so special in ToI, to which he replied, that it has a Bridge column in it.

It was my turn to move on the post now. I was well kitted and along with a patrol moved early morning to Patrol base No 2 in the Darshak Complex. I stayed there for 48 hrs to acclimatize since it was a sudden climb of 3000 feet. All moves in the glacier take place with link patrols. I later moved to Zulu post with a patrol and the route was a breathtaking view. Just prior to reaching my post, I had to climb an ice wall which was nothing less than 60 ft high with a steep gradient of almost 75 degree. Use of crampons assisted me to climb that with ease. The first day at 20000 ft in minus 45 degree C, got across in high morale. I was greeted by the boys at the post. We had no flowing water. Only solid Ice or fresh snow. One 5 Kg empty egg powder tin was always kept over a burning stove inside the snow hut wherein fresh snow would be stored so as to create drinking water as well as for washing purpose. The appetite goes down and you tend to lose weight in very short duration. Quality packed and pre prepared meals were available in abundance but always avoided. The only thing I enjoyed consuming was *"Frootie juice"* and that too use to be frozen and had to take a dip in the boiling water inside the egg powder tin. Snowfall at times would be continuous thus covering the entire helipad. Once, I recollect in emergency need of helicopter landing on our post, we used coffee powder to mark the "H" on our Helipad. Every post on Siachin had a dog (Tibetan mastiff). They were local and could sense as to who is the Boss. They always followed the Patrol emanating from the post and returned back with it. We were issued "5 star chocolate bars" in ration but they would be as hard as your femur bone. I used to keep two of them in my jacket pocket and every morning on coming out of my snow hut, I would find Mr canine waiting and would invariably put his paws over my shoulder and wouldn't budge till I put a chocolate bar in his mouth. A sweet bone made his day.

A Snow Mobile was present at my post which assisted me to visit the nearby posts however; it resulted into a catastrophe one evening. I and Havaldar Bhagat Singh were travelling at night. It was a moon lit night and the snow mobile was making reasonable noise in the rarified environment. Suddenly we were attacked with a burst of tracer ammunition fire from the Pakistani OP- 1 Post. We were totally caught unaware and lost control of the snow mobile and fell across in the snow. When it got all quiet, I solely got up and looked for Havaldar Bhagat who was seen nowhere. While I was walking slowly, I felt as if I have hit something with my foot. It was Bhagat's hand. I gave all my energy left in me to get him out to breathe first and thereafter we looked for the snow mobile which was traced but embedded in snow. Both of us shouted *"Jai Bajrang Bali ki jai"* and suddenly that force x infinity helped us to get the machine out which even started in first ignition. Such situations at times make one start believing in God Almighty existing in all forms and everywhere. On reaching the post both of us had bad chill blains in hand and feet. A lesson learnt that night was not to use snow mobile on a moon lit night or a starry night.

The time was running out and we would be soon told to de induct from the post when I and my buddy one day came under heavy artillery shelling of Pakistanis. They were firing air bursts and I could make out that the OP-2 was observing our movement and engaging us. Unfortunately, my buddy got shrapnel in his ankle and was in sheer pain. If he was not moved out from snow exposure could have been very dangerous. At that point there was no one around. I took chance and ran towards him and started to pull him to cover in an Ice cave. I too got hit on my back but it was very small shrapnel of an arty airburst too. Inside the Ice cave, which is considered to be the safest in such situation, I opened the first aid bag and gave a shot of pain killer to my buddy and self too. Later after last light, we came into our snow hut and were attended by the nursing assistant and warmed up to senses. The Brigade Commander was in know of things and wanted me at Zulu post for some more time and assigned me an important task. The task does not need elaboration but I happened to stay on the post for 102 days in total viz-a-viz 90 days for rest. I was happy to have performed the task well and to the satisfaction of my superiors.

102 days on post had made me a zombie with long beard and not having changed my dress for the entire duration. Our Battalion was relieved by 12 Jammu and Kashmir Rifles battalion in Mar 1990. The first set of reliving troops reached my post and I was lucky enough to get a helicopter lift to the base camp avoiding such a long walk down. The moment I reached the cheetah hut, a jeep was waiting for me and when I reached my room, a barber. He played merry hell with my beard and hair; thereafter I was virtually given a sizzling hot water bath to bring back the human in me alive. I was happy to comprehend all signs and words. We packed up subsequently and moved back to Partapur where the Brigade headquarters was there. We had a Sainik Sammelan (Public address) by the Brigade Commander and were presented mementoes. We got the recognition for being the first battalion to be de inducted from Siachin without a war fatal casualty. The stupendous performance of the battalion is in a way a direct reflection of an excellent command of Col Pratap Singh, CO. His Command tenure was over now and received his posting orders. The Second in Command, Lt Col DR Choudhary picked up his rank of Col and took over the reins from Col Pratap singh.

The romance of battle apart, is there a way forward? Efforts to de-militarize the Glacier in 1989 and in 1992 were set-aside after long rounds of Indo-Pak negotiations. It was politicians then –and not soldiers, who had made the fight over the glacier region a matter of national honour and prestige and were in no mood to compromise and suffer a loss of face domestically. Today, a military solution to the Siachen dispute can be found if only both sides agree to a formal demarcation of their positions, as it exists today – called the AGPL or the Actual Ground Position Line – as was done with the LoC, with joint patrolling by both sides. This could include first a disengagement and not withdrawal, for a reasonably long period that would take the Siachen dispute away from the public eye.

Our next three months passed in recuperating at Leh airfield where we had camped. Our move schedule was also issued by Army headquarters and we were to move to Amritsar, Punjab by Nov/Dec 1990. Towards the end of my tenure on the post, I had penned down a poem on my Battalions service to the nation at Siachin Glacier as under..........

Land of Wind, Chill and Thrill!!
(my experience in Siachin Glacier.... The highest battle field on earth)

"*Miles and miles away from home,*

Leaps and bounds above my dome,

Enclosed in the hills where Sun barely shone,

However, Thrill befits the environment of its own!!

Folds in mountains and rivulets flowing by,

Intense the passion with ecstasy filled eyes,

For a moment sunshine, then a nimbus cloak,

Thunder strikes and the silence broke!!

Soldiers covered from head to toe,

Not exposing a pore for Chill to go,

Still shivering but has taken a vow,

Lay my life, but never stoop low!!

Nature's misgivings or a Paki attack,
Well geared to deter any such nefarious threats,
The gruesome aura and our undaunted souls,
Always alert and marching for the goal!!
Complete devotion and no frills,
In this land of....
"Wind, Chill and Thrill"

Col Madhur Goyal, SM(retd)

Chapter VII

The Spiritual and Cultural Land of Sikhs: Amritsar

"Like All Great Travellers, I Have Seen More Than I Remember and Remember More Than I Have Seen."

– Benjamin Disraeli

The de induction of battle hardened soldiers from the highest battle field on Earth culminated at Amritsar, the spiritual and cultural land of Sikhs. It was Aug 1990 and the humidity factor was at its peak. The battalion being from Jat Regiment was ideally placed under 54 Brigade also known as Dograi brigade (3rd Battalion the Jat Regiment then under 54 Brigade advanced and captured Dograi town part of Lahore District in 1965 war). The unit in spite of its actual age had grown up a bit too early and started to compete with units of 50 years vintage and above.

We all have heard a great deal about Amritsar. The name is nothing new and intricately linked with the history of Sikhism; Amritsar is amongst the most esteemed cities of the world. It was founded as recently as the 16th century. Its name is an imitative of the "Amrit Sarovar" (pool of nectar) amidst which stands the Golden Temple, the most sacred of Sikh shrines. Accounts suggest that Guru Amardas purchased the land from Emperor Akbar and decided to build a tank at the site. Following his death, it was completed by Guru

Ramdas and also came to be known as Chak Ramdas or Guru ka Chak.

Some of the oldest markets in Amritsar, notably Guru ka Bazaar, date back to his time. The structure of the Golden Temple was initiated by Guru Arjan Dev while Guru Hargobind, who accorded the religion a martial temper, built the Akal Takht in 1606. Amritsar has a rich history encompassing various mythical and historical narratives including the epic Ramayana. Durgiana Mandir(temple), an important religious pilgrimage of The Hindus is situated just a few yards away from Railway Station. This city of Amritsar is pious, as it was visited by Lord Rama, Maryada Parshotam at the time of Ashavmegh Yagh. Lov & Kush spent their childhood along with their mother Mata Sita at the Ashram of Maharishi Balmiki at Ram Tirath. King Ishvaku Grandson of Surya Devta (Sun God) performed a number of Yagyas on this land. The idea to build Shree Durgiana Mandir as it stands today was the brain child of "Gur Shai Mal Kapoor", a great visionary and religious minded person. The foundation stone of the temple was laid down by Pandit Madan Mohan Malviya in 1924 on Ganga Dashmi day. Shree Durgiana Committee (Regd) runs varied service units to extend help & succor to the needy and the deserving. The Gobindgarh Fort and Ram Bagh were built by Maharaja Ranjit Singh, the founder of the Sikh Empire. While the Jallianwala Bagh continues to be the most evocative monument to India's freedom struggle. Also a Centre of flourishing industry since its foundation, Amritsar is famed for its textiles, particularly shawls, and for its carpets. Amritsar has gained tremendous popularity for its epicurean traditions; especially the *dhabas* (roadside eatery) that toss out, amongst an endless list of delicacies, irresistible kulchas, chola-bhaturas, tandoori chicken and fried fish. Amritsar has all the makings of a well-rounded tourist destination; its ancient legends, historical monuments, places of worship, old bazaars, theatre traditions and colourful festivals all serve as a window to its robust past. Visits to the India-Pakistan border at Wagah is an absolute delight, while baking bread or celebrating Diwali with the dwellers of this hospitable city is unparalleled. Hall bazar is one of the most important shopping complexes of Amritsar. You can get a variety of jewelry, books, Pakistani jootis, handicraft items like phulkari and readymade garments available here in plenty.

It was time for my wedding bells. Ringing....Ringing....Ringing......

During my short leave on de induction from Glacier tenure and recuperating at Leh airfield camp site, I was summoned by my sister to report at Kolkatta since quite a few matrimonial alliances had been received and I was being given the honor of final choice. My pledge taken @ Kolkatta after the culmination of 3rd SAF Games seems to be materializing to a logical conclusion. I took the first flight and reached the city of Joy once again and the first few days were really enthralling in the company of my sister and her family after the grueling tenure of Siachin. Lot of information was exchanged and finally reached the brass talk of finalizing my matrimonial alliance. Needless to say, I got bowed to the bio data of *"Reena Gupta"*, residing at Kolkata itself. My sister too had top listed her amongst the rest and then she called up her mom to arrange a meeting of both the families. They resided at "Garden Reach" railway apartments as Reena's dad was a very senior officer in the South Eastern railway with its Headquarters at Kolkatta.

Meeting Reena for the first time, made me feel like a man of no words. This generally happens when your wife is in front of you..... It happened too early for me probably. Another strong indication of a permanent bond!! Subsequently all went well and both families had approved of the alliance. We met again and again till I came back home with a *"lipstick on my collar"* (My sister showed it to me which indeed made me blush). Finally, Dad and Mom arrived from Kenya on a long visit to solemnize the engagement ritual and subsequently followed by the marriage on 26 Sep 1990 at their ancestral place, Gurgaon. We had a great honeymooning holiday at Andaman's group of Islands. We took a flight ex Delhi to Port Blair and spent an exotic and fun filled holiday at Andaman's. We got to know each other much better and returned back via Kolkatta paying respects to her parents. Finally, my declaration of Kolkatta *"Dilwale dulhaniya le jayenge"* was fulfilled and *"Dilwale Kolkatta wali dulhaniya le gaye"*. Mission accomplished!!

I had already spoken to my CO seeking his blessing to get my wife in station (customary in Armed forces). The day arrived when Reena and Self de boarded the train and were welcomed by all officers and ladies at the railway station. The Battalion's Pipe band was present playing the favorite military tunes at the platform and a table of eats and tea was well laid out. I was aware of the customs but Reena was totally spellbound being from a civilian background. My entity had changed...... I was no more a bachelor and now, one amongst the married officers. We had an invitation waiting the same evening for our dining in party at the officer's mess where we both were officially welcomed by all officers and ladies of the battalion.

As days passed by, Reena learnt the customs and traditions of a Jat paltan and more so being a fauji officer's wife. Since one swallow doesn't make a summer, the battalion had to move but not too far, within the jurisdiction of Amritsar only. The Punjab terrorism was still in existence after the Operation Bluestar. We moved to Wagah border and got deployed on the DCB (Ditch cum Bund) linear defenses. It was difficult separation for the newlyweds but generally I used to get a weekend off courtesy CO's human heart inside a battle hardened soldiers body. With passage of time we got meshed with the fraternity and established our entity as Captain and Mrs Madhur Goyal. There was no looking back thereafter........ Reena became a railway extension booking counter of the Battalion, courtesy her dad. In Army as we know, move of officers take place at very short notice and it's very difficult to get confirmed Rail reservation in authorized class. However, we ensured that every officer and families of the unit will get privileged to this service.

The peak winters of Amritsar made us all shiver. Notwithstanding we were veterans of Siachin and got out easily out unscathed even at − 50 degrees C but feeling the pinch here!! True, the type of clothing, equipment and additional resources for central heating facility was available in abundance which was void here being in plains and a peace station. My parents visited us for a couple of months since I was generally away in the forward area and they could give company to Reena. My parents loved to travel and explore new places; invariably they would just move out of the house at 10.00 am and return back by early evening. Within a span of a month they knew Amritsar like the back of their hand. In one of the parties at the officer's mess, it was decided to plan a get together at Wagah border and witness the *"Beating retreat ceremony"*. My parents along with Reena were also travelling and it was a much awaited moment for me.

Wagah is a village that is 32 kilometers from Amritsar in India and 24 kilometers from Lahore in Pakistan. The village is located at the Radcliffe line, the demarcation line that was drawn when India was partitioned. Wagah lies 600 meters west of the line. In Pakistan the border crossing is known as Wagha border. However, in India, the border crossing is known as Atari border, named after the village Atari that lies 500 meters from the line within the Indian boundary. It is here at the Wagah-Atari border that the Indian Border Security Force (BSF) and Pakistan Rangers (PR) display a tradition that has been followed two hours before sunset every day since 1959: the lowering of the flags ceremony. The ceremony begins with a puff parade by the soldiers from both the sides, and ends with perfectly coordinated lowering of the flags of both the countries. This 'beating retreat' border ceremony is one of the most witnessed military ceremonies that attract crowds from both the sides of the border, as well as international tourists. The boot thumping, eye-to-eye stares, the martial cries, and the overall viciousness of the ceremony makes it engaging for the crowd. The ceremony that was started as a generosity wave turned overly competitive and aggressive now.

The complete entourage of "Twenty Jat" arriving from Amritsar was present, while they were all busy watching the soldiers thumping their feet, I was more eager to look for my wife as to where she was, it got worrisome for me since I could see my parents sitting but Reena was nowhere in sight. Suddenly, I felt a soft hand patting my right shoulder, I turned back only to find my wife, Reena, standing there with a small steel dabba (tiffin box) containing some *"Laddus"* (sweet balls). She was blushing as if she was hiding something from me. I said, come on Reena, what's it?? She said very softly close to my ear that, *"I am expecting a baby"*. I was thunderstruck and didn't know how to react. Just babbled a few words with no connect. Then, the face changed colours reflecting the happiness of a father in making. She felt my emotions and soon I found my CO in near vicinity watching us. He probably got the news through his wife but did not disclose it in public. He just said, *"So Madhur, it's nice that you are taking a break for a week. Go and look after Mrs Goyal and your parents"*. I was indeed taken by surprise. That evening I returned back to Amritsar with them only.

We had a professional Golf course within our Cantt limits, "Panther Golf Club". The functioning of the Club was one of my Battalions responsibilities. I was made the Assistant Secretary while my CO was the Secretary. Since CO was a busy appointment, I was the man Friday at the club. Here I learnt the difference between woods, Irons, wedges and putters or else for me earlier, a driver was the one who only drives a vehicle. I started playing for leisure just to be confident enough to shout at a foursome playing, *"Good shot sir!!"* I remember having organized a National level Golf tournament, "OCM Open". We welcomed a few of the famous National Golf stars. Three days of fun and frolic ended with a farewell dinner and prize distribution. The prizes were sponsored by the OCM Industries.

All good things come to an end, due to ascendency in Punjab militancy, the battalion was ordered to move to Tarn Taran and Majitha district of Punjab for area domination. Although yearning to be away from the loved ones but professionally it was a very fruitful exposure. I recollect the day specific at Tarn Taran Battalion Headquarters location performing the duties as Adjutant, my *RP NCO* (Regimental police Non Commissioned Officer) informed me that a local Sikh middle aged man wanted to meet me in person. He wanted to share some intelligence inputs on terrorists with me only. However, he said that they are skeptical about this guy!! I told him to get the man in and you be just outside the office with door kept open and be alert in case of any eventuality. The guy was tall and well-built unlike a normal village guy. He said that he's heard about our battalion accepting surrenders from terrorists. I acknowledged however added that the individual must be in possession of a weapon and be a listed terrorist as per police records. He said that, one of his relative wants to surrender. I asked him the terrorists name and he gave it out without any hesitation. I checked the list of terrorists available with me and found his name but more astonishing was the photo next to it was matching exactly with the guy sitting opposite me……. I understood his contention and called my RP NCO inside the office and told him to go along with a QRT (Quick Reaction Team) and get the weapon of the terrorist sitting in front of me. Both the RP NCO and the terrorist were spell bound on my statement. The mystery was solved and the terrorist just went out of the Unit gate where he had hid his "AK 56 Rifle" hidden in a bush and handed over to my RP NCO.

Mr KPS Gill, DGP Punjab Police visited us to compliment for the magnificent action by our unit to contain the terrorist activities in the region being a hot bed. A pile of 26 terrorists had planned to surrender to our unit and the DGP wanted to give a big publicity to the event. It was planned at our Officers mess at Tarn Taran which was telecast live on national and vernacular TV channels too. The military training directorate at Army Headquarters keeps experimenting on the latest trends. They wanted Infantry and Armoured corps officers to proceed on cross attachment for a year with each other units so as to build confidence in the event of balloon goes up and exhibit synergized effort on the battle field as "Infantry tank cooperation'. This was the first of its kind and I was the lucky one chosen to get an exposure with "76 Armored Regiment" at Bikaner, Rajasthan. Since I would not like to break your chain of thought here, therefore, I will explain my exploits of Bikaner in the next chapter and will continue presently at Amritsar only from the time of my return from Bikaner after a breathtaking tenure I had with the "Black Dungarees". Breaking news, Reena and Self returned from Bikaner as *"threesome"*. My Son Madhav, baby in arms was with us now at Amritsar.

Immediately on my return I was earmarked for my JC Course (Junior Command) at Mhow, Indore in Madhya Pradesh. *"JC aya!"* Sounds like *"Piya ghar aya"* (Earmarked for JC Course is akin to arrival of husband back home), Reena and Madhav accompanied me for the course. I once heard someone say that Mhow shopkeepers make a lot of money, thanks to Army wives. "Dohars", "Chanderi sarees", "smocking dresses" and special Mhow "embroidery saree" are the things that the Army wives love to hoard. The traders of the tiny Mhow market eagerly await the arrival of every JC course. The three months fly by way too fast. Many of us were wondering how the wives will take care of the baby (babies, in some cases) alone, without any help from husbands. Many of us kept thinking of how they would pass time in that sleepy town. We all think of how we'll be able to pack all the stuff we shopped for into those tiny bags we brought. Time simply flies! And before we realize, it's all over. We made some glorious friends, revel in the fact that we consumed less alcohol and more notepads, and took back some awesome memories with us. Hasta la vista Mhow! It was a great blissful togetherness and professionally satiating too since I returned to unit acquiring an "Instructors" grading which has recognition of its own.

There was a change of guard once again in my battalion and this time Col DR Choudhary, CO received his posting orders on completion of his command tenure and Col Pradeep Sharma was the new Tiger in chair. A very refined and soft spoken officer with whom it was a pleasure to talk. The unit had also got its move orders and this time we were again on an operational role to check the menace of Insurgency in the North eastern state of Assam. The rolling stock was placed and slowly steadily the unit was busy packing up and loading simultaneously. My father-in-law helped the battalion by getting the "taking over time of rolling stock" extended by a few days or else the battalion would have to pay extensive demurrage charges. It was a noble gesture by him and accepted by Indian Railways since the unit was deeply involved in Punjab terrorism and had no time to pack up so soon bringing back the bond between the two even closer.

"Traveling – It Leaves You Speechless, Then Turns You into a Storyteller."

– IBN Battuta

Chapter VIII

Tally Ho!! Armoured Corps: Bikaner

"You hit somebody with your fist and not with your fingers spread".

– Heinz Guderian

Post marriage, this was my first transfer with wife, Reena, out of the battalion. We both had bunch of questions in mind about an Armoured regiment while the train kept chugging towards Bikaner. All she knew was, they have tanks to fight with, where as I was a little richer in knowledge perhaps. We retired soon being an overnight train and got up early to see barren desert land, sand-dunes, grazing camels, cactus plants, tribes and settlements of desert inhabitants. The golden rays of sun sparkling out of the sand particles during sunrise were like a cherry on the cake. Travelling by train was more like being on a desert safari. We had earlier despatched our household luggage by a truck whereas we were carrying the essentials and my two wheeler scooter with us. We reached Bikaner and were received by the unit representatives of our new Regiment "Seventy Six Armoured".

Bikaner is home to one of the only two models of the biplane used by the British during World War I. They were presented by the British to Maharaja Ganga Singh, then ruler of the city. Another unique aspect about Bikaner is the sand dunes that are scattered throughout the district, especially from the north-east down to the southern area. Bikaner is situated in the northern region of Rajasthan. One of the earlier established cities, Bikaner still displays its ancient affluence through palaces and forts, built of red sandstone, that have withstood the passage of time. The city boasts of some of the world's best riding camels and is aptly nicknamed 'camel country'. It is also home to one of the world's largest camel research and breeding farms; as well as being known for having its own unique temple dedicated to Karni Mata at Deshnok, called the Rats Temple. The origins of Bikaner can be traced back to 1488 when a Rathore prince, Rao Bikaji, founded the kingdom. Legend has it that Bikaji, one of Rao Jodhaji's five sons, left his father's Durbar in annoyance after an insensitive remark from his father, the illustrious founder of Jodhpur. Bikaji travelled far and when he came upon the wilderness called Jangladesh, he decided to set up his own kingdom and transformed it into an impressive city.

The regiment was actually located in Udasar cantt which was not a KLP (Key location plan) for an armoured regiment. Hence, the tenure was considered as soft field station. We had arrived at the officer's mess and a well-furnished single officer's accommodation was earmarked for us till the time we hired a house in civil area (on reimbursement basis). I let Reena sort out the logistics and I took some time off to pay a visit to the office complex and report my arrival to the Adjutant and also meet other officers too. It took no time to make friends here as I found a few likeminded officers who were bachelors though but gelled from day one perfectly. Being a Saturday, all officers arrived at the mess for a beer session which lasted till 3.00 Pm followed by some sumptuous biryani and raita (fruit salad mixed in curd). Reena didn't mind the delay since we were already residing in the mess and she was busy munching often and on due to her state of pregnancy. Finally, I settled for an independent house fulfilling our need and close enough to the regiment.

Armoured corps is considered modern-day cavalry. If cavalries brought speed and mobility to the battlefields of yesteryears, tanks play the role in today's battles. The Indian Army's 3,000 plus tanks are divided among some 60 armoured regiments; each one with about 50 tanks and other vehicles. The regiments are divided in three sabre squadrons and one headquarters squadron. Each of these sabre's squadrons—Alpha, Bravo and Charlie—are equipped with 14 tanks. The headquarters squadron is an administrative unit and has three tanks, including that of the commandant who is an officer of the rank of colonel.

During the tenure of my cross attachment, my training was divided into four phases encompassing driving and maintenance, gunnery, communications, culminating in the tactical phase of outdoor exercise with troops. The bonding between the men and their tanks is reflected in the interesting names given to their machines. I recollect the tank commanded by the legendary Lt Col Ardeshir Tarapore, who was awarded Param Vir Chakra for his bravery in the 1965 war, was called Kooshab. "We are nothing without our equipment. Tank is a fighting member of our unit and hence it should also have a name. That is the sentiment behind naming tanks" says an Armoured Corps General. I was fascinated by tanks and affectionately called them monsters. Monster because of the shock and the effect that it has on enemy psyche, It is a Great War machine. In fact while at Indian Military Academy, my choice of Arms was "Armoured Corps" as first choice although I was allotted "Infantry".

The rapid expansion of the Army's armoured corps started soon after the 1965 war with Pakistan. It was a war of mobile warfare and tank battles. This was also the war in which we realized that Pakistan is potentially our number one enemy. After the war it was felt that we were dolefully short of equipment and tanks. So, 1966 onwards there was rapid expansion of armoured corps. The Armoured Corps provide the definitive punch to the enemy with highly calibrated firepower of pin point accuracy from lethal mean machines, namely - the tanks. The assault if well-coordinated has always left a gaping hole in the enemy and dealt a death blow. The Armoured Corps has often proven to be the decisive arm which has swung the tide of many battles for armies in their favour around the world and the same holds true for the Indian Army.

I switched over to the accouterments of "Seventy Six Armoured" since it was customary and made me comfortable enough as part of the family. I was now a "Black Dungaree" warrior with a tilted black beret over my head. It was not so easy though. I had to earn it in true spirit. My day would start with physical exercise followed by maintenance parade in tank garages till 10.00am. I was briefed on each and every part of a tank by rolling, crawling, creeping over and underneath a tank. We had modified and up gunned Vijayant's and this monster was indeed some mean machine. I had a deep rooted exposure for three weeks on the tank with one week each as a driver, gunner and radio operator. This raised my confidence level to speak about a battle tank if required. The regiment was preparing for a Combat Group exercise wherein I was now part of "B" Squadron with Major Singh as my Squadron Commander. When the regiment was inducting into the exercise area, Major Singh was en route from outstation leave and would take another two days to join us. I was the Boss for a while and felt elated. Holi festival (Indian festival of colours) was just a day ahead and I had quite a few Jat community boys in my Squadron and I visualized being from Jat Regiment as to how they feel about Holi. Since my Squadron was in a "Harbour" and any further action was unlikely to take place until Maj Singh joined up so I took a command decision of lighting Holi that night as a customary ritual (burning firewood and dancing around it) and issue a tot of Rum to all ranks in the Squadron. It was a great evening and next day was Holi festival. The boys wanted to make merry in whatever capacity and played with colours. However, all good things come to an end when the Commandant and the Second in Command drove into my location and found the celebration in making. I could make out from the face of the Commandant as to how furious he was. He directed his entire wrath towards the Risaldar Sahab, a senior JCO (Junior Commissioned officer) who was a seasoned Armoured corps soldier since his inception in service. I could feel the pinch of each word hitting me like an arrow since it was my decision and I was to be blamed for it. However, both the officers returned back to the RHQ (Regimental Headquarters) and a little while later I found the regiment TO (Technical Officer) arriving at my location stating with a smile that the Commandant wants me to sleep for the night in this location since Maj Singh is joining up tomorrow for the exercise. This episode was a bitter pill to digest, nevertheless gave me enough reasons to prove myself.

During the course of exercise, I was tested by the Commandant on my skills for the three trades as driver, gunner and operator of his tank. He was spell bound to see my performance in that short period and ensured to make a mention about it in the summing up exercise in front of the Brigade Commander. Armoured regiment is indeed equipment heavy and one is bound to make mistakes or the equipment lets you down. Having gained the trust and belief of the seniors of the unit, I was given an independent task this time. My wife, Reena, was at a later stage of pregnancy and I was detailed to proceed with 14 training tanks of the regiment to the ITC (Individual training cycle) location. All tanks were loaded on tank transporters and we commenced our journey on Jaipur highway. After 20 Km we had to turn left leaving the highway but the Tank transporter trailer carrying the Tank could not negotiate the turn and got stuck thereby holding the traffic on the busy Jaipur Highway. Taking expert views from my seasoned JCOs, I took the decision of dismounting the tank off the trailer so that it makes easy for the Tatra truck to turn and thereafter the tank could be loaded again. The driver cranked the engine of the tank and resumed unloading it on reverse gear. As luck would have it, the driver could not control the rolling back of tank which went a bit wayward and the left track of the tank ran over the motorcycle of CMP (Corps of Military police) pilot. The state of motorcycle is not worth mentioning and can be well understood as to what may happen if a 40 ton weight rolls over it. It was like another shot in my arm but this time I was not blaming myself. I took my rover jeep and immediately proceeded to the Regiment and found the Commandant taking class of officers being a Saturday as a routine. He saw me at the entrance and was worried!! He asked me, *"Ahh!! Madhur, I hope all is well with Reena"*. I said, *"Sir, nothing wrong on that front but......blah!! Blah!!...."* I rattled out the entire incident. He thought for 30 secs and put his arm around my shoulder and said, "I have sent you for training just concentrate on it and make the boys sweat and learn. Don't worry on this issue." He directed the technical officer to take a separate vehicle and load the CMP motorcycle and get it in the LRW of our regiment. That was the last I heard about the incident. My ITC terminated and I returned back with all the tanks safely and was surprised to meet the CMP Pilot a few days later who seemed to be very happy to see me and told me that his motorcycle is absolutely fit and as good as new. This episode indeed cleared the cobwebs in my head about professionalism. I found armoured corps officers full of resilience and with a big heart too.

Reena was expecting any day now and the Commandant had instructed that a jeep would be parked at all times at my house just in case to take her to the Military Hospital in emergency. Finally it was 02 September 1991, a pious day of "Janmashtmi" (Indian festival commemorating the birth of Lord Krishna), my son was born at the Military hospital. It was evening time and was raining. In fact I later learnt that the Commandant of hospital came to know about the birth of my son and even light heartedly told his staff that as customary the baby can be brought in the adhoc temple created on janmashtmi and made to lie down in the "jhoola" (Swing) like baby Krishna. We named him "Madhav"(another name of Lord Krishna). My parents were also present at Bikaner during the delivery time; all were overjoyed with the birth of my first child. I remember there was a party in our officers' mess that evening and when they learnt about the news, it was like a yuletide. The Second in Command and a few officers along with my squadron boys in one big truck arrived at the Hospital. The sentry on duty would not permit entry to any of them to which the second in command made a call to the commandant of the Hospital. Finally, only a few were permitted to enter the premises and Reena's room window was opened from where she could wave to all of them and convey her gratitude for all the best wishes and blessings she received. Days passed by providing strength to both the mother and child.

The most important battle worthy test for an armoured officer and his mean machines are at the field firing ranges where real battlefield conditions are simulated to train soldiers in the entire spectrum of war-fighting. Our Regiment proceeded to "MFFR" (Mahajan Field Firing Ranges) as an annual feature of training with actual firing of live ammunition. I was now given the charge of "A" Squadron since the Squadron Commander was a services football player and was away for about six months. The initial setting up of camp, ensuring safety and security of arms, ammunition and equipment hold paramount importance. Regular cleaning of tank barrels, Small arms cleaning is a regular feature. One day the Commandant called me to his office and said, "*Madhur, the Corps Commander is visiting us on Monday and your "A" Squadron will be firing and carrying out the Battle run. Therefore, plan and do well*". I was lost for words and said, "*Sir, I'm an Infantry officer and unknowingly may commit a mistake. You must let your permanent officer undertake this task since it's a prestige issue for the regiment"*. The Commandant was not too amused with my reply and said, *"Are you not confident enough??"* I apologized for my words and accepted the challenge and started off with my preparation of radio orders and firing practices. As I said earlier, we had up graded Vijayant tanks with TFCS (Tank firing control system) and GLNS (Gyro land navigation system). These additions had made the tank highly accurate in firing and mapping skills. The Up graded guns from 105 mm to 155 mm made the Vijayants even more lethal. Finally the day arrived and yours truly let no stone unturned and ensured all derelicts available were blown out of proportion. The spectacular demonstration of fire power and maneuver showcased the capabilities, proficiency and operational preparedness of 76 Armoured regiment. The ear-deafening thunder of "A" Squadron Tanks which unleashed their lethal and accurate fire power at the MFFR left the Corps Commander awestruck. When it was all over, the Corps commander wanted to meet me personally. I came closer to him and he shook my hand, I could feel the warmth and strength of a soldier in that handshake. He asked me, *"76 Armoured is a new raising, are you an original officer of the regiment or came from some other regiment?"* I was not expecting this question from him, however, I answered, *"Sir, I am an Infantry officer from 20 Jat, on cross attachment!!"* I could feel the handshake getting weak and melting into sweat. The Commandant took on thereafter and spoke a few good words about me. He finally smiled and gave a pat on my back and left.

Although this incident was the culmination of my tenure with "seventy six" and I returned back to Amritsar and joined my parent unit "20 Jat". It was even more pleasing to learn that "seventy six" had also received its move orders and the complete unit was coming to Amritsar and would be stationed at "Khasa cantt" near Wagah border. Here I would like to reiterate a true professional example of "Infantry tank cooperation" which became a live case study for the Indian army officers as visualized by the brains who perceived this concept of cross attachment between Infantry and Armoured Regiments/Battalions.

An Operation Alert was announced by the Divisional Headquarters as part of an annual training event. All Units took up defences along the DCB (Ditch cum Bund). I had returned back from my "JC" (Junior Command) Course and was performing the duties of "C" Company Commander in my unit, 20 Jat. During OP Alert, the Counter attack armour sqadron was to pass through my company locality and as per set drills and SOP, the defending infantry company commander is responsible to ensure safe passage of the armour column maintaining complete stealth and correct direction or else the counter attack may fail and causing a major catastrophe. It so happened that it was none other than my own "A" Squadron which was to pass through my own "C" company. It was a treat to watch when my 20 Jat boys found me sitting on the Squadron commander's tank and guiding the complete tank column. In humour, the Squadron commander also stated, "Why don't you only lead the squadron into attack? You can do it as well as any other armoured corps officer". This part of OP Alert became an important discussion point during the summing up after the training event.

> *"...It is a proud privilege to be a soldier – a good soldier ... with discipline, self-respect, pride in his unit and his country, a high sense of duty and obligation to comrades and to his superiors, and a self-confidence born of demonstrated ability."*
>
> *– George S. Patton Jr.*

Chapter IX

The Land of Bihu: Assam

The battalion had almost three and a half years tenure at Amritsar; however the maximum period was spent in OP RAKSHAK and in battle fatigues in spite of being a peace station. I was however a bit lucky to have got a decent opportunity to serve with 76 armoured Regiment at Bikaner and undergoing the JC Course at Mhow. The military special train was all loaded and courtesy the Indian railways, the unit got respite of a week to ensure proper loading and tie up its loose ends. We commenced our journey in Apr 1994, It was again a long journey however, I was looking ahead for the train to its scheduled halt at Saharanpur(My home town) en route where my parents would be coming over to the station to meet us (main attraction being the grandchild, Madhav). It was a halt of 30 mins and a very emotional one. Mom had brought lot of eats to cater for all officers and ladies in the train which really helped us to keep our taste buds active. Three days of long and arduous journey which we had earlier witnessed. Therefore, it was not very enthusiastic though. Before I go further with my journey of Assam, I take this opportunity to acquaint the readers about this fascinating state and the reasons we were inducted here for.......

Assam is the largest north eastern state that contains three of six physiographic divisions of India – The Northern Himalayas (Eastern Hills), The Northern Plains (Brahmaputra plain) and Deccan Plateau (Karbi Anglong). It is famous for its abundant forest resources and is remarkably rich in Orchid species and the Foxtail orchid (Rhynchostylis retusa) also known as the "Kopou Phul" is the State Flower of Assam. The wildlife sanctuaries of which the two **UNESCO** World Heritage sites-the Kaziranga National Park and the Manas Wildlife Sanctuary are most famous. Kaziranga is home to the fast-disappearing Indian one-horned rhinoceros which has also been recognized as the State Animal of Assam. The state bird of Assam is the white-winged wood duck. The Barak and the Brahmaputra rivers with their innumerable tributaries are the source of water here. Assam has the single largest tea growing area in the world, constituting around one-seventh of the global tea production. It has its own variety Camellia assamica. The state accounts for over 50 per cent in the country's overall tea production. Assam Silk denotes the three major types of indigenous wild silks produced here—Golden Muga Silk, White Pat and warm Eri Silk. The state is a major producer of crude oil and natural gas in India too.

Assam is India's gateway to the Northeast and acts as a vital link for trade with Southeast Asian countries. It is well connected by rail, road, ports and airports. The State has adopted numerous investor-friendly policies to attract investments & accelerate industrial development. Talking about Guwahati in general, it is a 'melting pot' of different cultures, faith and ethnicities and is truly a symbolization of *"unity in a great diversity"*. It can rightfully be termed as a Mini India in this northeastern heartland. People from across the seven states as well as from the rest of India call it home. Even though it cannot be compared to any metro cities in terms of infrastructure and wealth, herein lays the true spirit of an independent and united India.

We reached Guwahati and unloading commenced. Entire unit was located within the transit camp which was barely 50 m walk from the railway station. The advance party had already tied up the transport for our further move to Sibsagar town which would be our

Battalion Headquarters location. Sibsagar is historically important part of Assam, lying East of Jorhat. Being the capital of the former rulers, the Ahoms, it has had a major impact in the culture. It is a town of decorated monuments and temples. Sibsagar gets the attention of history enthusiasts who've looked to understand the East of India better. It has also played a significant role in Indian history and therefore is an important destination for historical tourism. A few architectural marvels at Sibsagar are the Talatal Ghar, Rang Ghar and the Rangpur Palace. The initial reconnaissance was already carried out by the CO and four different locations were identified for the four rifle companies to establish piquets. But what was the necessity of forces in this area???

United Liberation Front of Assam (ULFA) was formed on April 7, 1979, by Bhimakanta Buragohain, Rajiv Rajkonwar alias Arabinda Rajkhowa, Golap Baruah alias Anup Chetia, Samiran Gogoi alias Pradip Gogoi, Bhadreshwar Gohain and Paresh Baruah at the Rang Ghar in Sibsagar to establish a "sovereign socialist Assam" through an armed struggle. Ulfa during its heydays (late eighties and nineties of the last century) was quite popular among many indigenous Assamese people of the Brahmaputra valley. Majority of the supporters felt that a powerful organisation was necessary to get the voice of a peripheral region heard in the corridors of power in Lutyen's Delhi. But gradually, the organization's undue emphasis on collection of money and weapons in the name of furthering the 'revolution' led to mindless violence throughout the state. It witnessed a period marked by growing disillusionment and anger amid its supporters. In their bloody conflict with the security agencies, many innocent people lost their lives and several thousands were permanently maimed. It is estimated that more than ten thousand local youths perished during that turbulent period. In the process, owing to the twin factors of increasing pressure by the security agencies and dwindling support among its core sympathisers, its importance in Assam has been steadily declined. In 1986 it launched a fund raising "campaign" across India by way of extortion. It then began to set up camps in Tinsukia and Dibrugarh but was soon banned. The Government of India (GOI) had classified it as a terrorist organisation and had banned it under the Unlawful Activities (Prevention) Act in 1990. Concurrently, GOI started military offensives against it, named "Operation Bajrang" November 1990, "Operation Rhino" September 1991, "Operation All Clear" December 2003 and "Operation Rhino 2" were led by the Indian Army. The anti-insurgency operations still continues at present under the Unified Command Structure.

Notwithstanding above, 20 Jat was fully geared up to tackle the menace of antinational activity in any form, be it insurgency or terrorist activity. The CO commenced his search and sweep operations in every nook and corner of the district which left an imprint on the locals as well as the ULFA activists to stay calm and quiet. I was the "A" Company Commander at "Charing village" almost 30 mins drive from Battalion Headquarters. Our families were located at Dinjan town which was also the location of our Divisional Headquarters. All the married officers with families had opted for separated family accommodation at Dinjan. We got a chance to visit Dinjan once a fort night and whenever we had organized a function at Sibsagar, the ladies would be escorted to the location. My wife Reena was expecting our second baby that was due anytime in Oct 1994. Since the time was nearing, CO permitted her to stay at my camp site where I had a decent accommodation. I still remember, whenever she would be travelling with the ladies in the jeep, the roads in that area were pretty undulating and the jeep would give a bumpy ride to the ladies and Mrs Moitra and Mrs Chandran would invariably keep supporting Reena so she doesn't get hurt at that crucial time. The ladies recommended naming the child "Jumpy" because of all the jumping the baby must have already done in the mother's womb. Going for the delivery in situ was not recommended and finally we took a decision of proceeding to Saharanpur, my hometown, where I would station her under my parents care and fixup a hospital where the delivery would take place.

We packed up and departed by "Lohit express" ex Guwahati which would take us straight to Saharanpur. All was going well when at late evening we found 12 dacoits with face masked and gloves on holding some improvised weapons entered the AC 2tier compartment and started to forcefully take away valuables from the passengers. I had a gold chain around my neck and Reena was also wearing one along with her "mangalsutra" apart from gold bangles. I told her to act fast and she gave me all that and I hid it inside my shoe. The rogues came into our compartment and asked for whatever valuables we had. I showed them my wallet which had Rs 300/- in cash which they snatched away. They saw Madhav sleeping on the lower berth and Reena was lying down on his side. Watching Reena in that later stage of pregnancy, they just asked her "What's in the bag? She opened the bag and threw all eatables on them in disgust. Somehow, they got scared and the other back up guy told the leader, "*Chal yaar, lafda ho jayega!!*" and they whisked away. About an hour later, the train stopped at some station in Bihar state where this information was communicated to the police authorities. I also spoke to my father-in-law at Kolkatta and he activated his railway police force to lodge an FIR. Next morning, breakfast was being served when Reena held my hand tight and pointed to the waiter serving breakfast and said, "*He was the guy yesterday evening*", I said "*how can you say so?*" She said "*look at the guys hand, he is wearing the same ring as the guy yesterday and his voice resembles too*". I started to wonder and as the train halted at the next station within a span of 15 mins, I reported to the RPF (Railway police force) giving reference of the loot and my father-in-law. The police immediately arrested the waiter without disclosing the fact as to who reported the matter. Although the train got delayed due to some hue and cry at the station but nevertheless the matter was with the police now. We reached Saharanpur almost 6 hours late but thanked our stars that all was well. After settling down Reena and selecting a Gynecologist for her supervision and a suitable nursing home close by, I returned back to the battalion location.

The battalion was tasked to plan for a seminar on "Ecology". CO was looking for a few known intellectuals in this field who could be invited and give a lecture. I was tasked to find a few and do the honors. I learnt about Dr Robin Bannerjee, Padma Shri awardee who was residing in a palatial bungalow in Golaghat, Assam. Dr Robin Banerjee was born on 12 August 1908 at Baharampur in West Bengal and received primary schooling at Santiniketan. He went on to pursue medical education at the prestigious Calcutta Medical College in Kolkata, and later at Liverpool (1934) and Edinburgh (1936). He had joined the Royal Navy in 1937 at Liverpool, and saw action in World War II. After the war, Banerjee decided to move back to India. In 1952, he visited Assam as a locum-tenens to a Scottish doctor. In 1952 he joined Chabua Tea Estate, Assam, as Chief Medical Officer, and later moved to the Dhansiri Medical Association, Bokakhat as the Chief Medical Officer. During a visit to Kaziranga National Park sometime in the 1950s, Banerjee fell in love with the wilds of Assam and decided to settle down at Golaghat, near Kaziranga. Banerjee's first film on the Kaziranga National Park (one of the most important refuges of the Indian rhinoceros) on Berlin TV in 1961 was one of the first widely distributed media items on the park to reach Western audiences. It also garnered him international recognition as a wildlife film-maker. He made 32 documentaries in his career as a film-maker, and was the recipient of 14 international awards. Banerjee remained a bachelor, and worked actively as an environmentalist besides his film-making career. Well known and loved among the local community as "Uncle Robin", he donated lands for setting up the local school, and health camps. He was particularly active regarding issues concerning Kaziranga National Park and was the founder of the non-governmental organization Kaziranga Wildlife Society, which actively protects the interests of the park. He was awarded the Padma Shri in 1971, an honorary Doctorate of Science from Assam Agricultural University (AAU) in 1991, and also an honorary Ph.D. from Dibrugarh University. A book based on his life and experiences has been written in Assamese named "Xeujia Xopunar Manuh".

I recollect my meeting with this genius at his residence. When my jeep entered his residential gate I was awestruck by the greenery and varied animals moving around the house. I was escorted inside the drawing room and told to wait. I saw an old and bald man walking slowly towards me in a very humble manner. He introduced himself and was very pleased to see me in my battle fatigues. While we were exchanging notes, I saw two huge pythons snaking their way towards the side of a sofa set. This scene was not palatable to me especially when they started to approach me. He said that the one ahead is named "Hema" being a female and the one behind is "Dharam" being male. He made some gesture and they rerouted their advance making me more comfortable and in peace. Dr Bannerjee took me to his basement where he had his treasure of those 32 spools of original films which he had shot. He said that National Geographic is ready to pay phenomenal amount to buy this treasure but he is not in a mood to part with it. The entire walls of his house were covered with wild life pictures or his certificates and awards. Finally, we had two small tots of whiskey and he accepted the invitation to give a talk for 30 mins during the seminar. We were all honored. I still remember his wonderful words on conservation of ecology.........

"Think twice before you kill an animal, think twice before you catch a butterfly, think before you cut a tree, because it may be the last member of the species that is left in the world."

Robin Banerjee died at his residence suffering from old age ailments on 6 August 2003. The pyre of Dr Banerjee was lit by his caretaker Jitoo Tamuli. The cremation was attended by Assam Minister of State for Tourism Ajanta Neog. The Golaghat district administration declared a half-holiday in memory of Banerjee.

Back to my bread and butter in fighting insurgency. One evening, I got an intelligence input of two ULFA activists planning to sabotage the oil pipeline of ONGC ex Nazira town towards a village falling in my area. I and my chosen QRT (Quick reaction team) moved at midnight short of the area where we parked our vehicle and moved with stealth close to the hut where they were putting up and furthering their plans. I gestured my boys to cordon the house and then I and my buddy broke open the door and entered the hut where two boys were lying down on the bed. Watching us they jumped up and tried to run towards the door. One was caught inside by my buddy but the second managed to jump out of the window where he was caught by the soldier waiting for him. They were interrogated in situ and with hesitation they took us to a bush where they dug for about a feet and took out a polybag containing two pistols and some ammunition. My "A" Company was the first one to apprehend two ULFA activists along with two pistols and few rounds. It was big news and the CO with brigade commander visited my Company location to convey "Shabash" to the boys. Our battalion had indeed exerted immense pressure in the entire jurisdiction which was proving fruitful.

I was in constant touch with my folks and Reena at Saharanpur. Although it's humanly impossible to give a precise date of delivery specially when it is considered to be a normal one. However, I applied for leave so as to be physically present next to my wife while she gifts me the second baby. I prayed like hell to be a daughter this time. All formalities were over of handing over to my Company second in command, and I reached Guwahati to board the train. This time I ensured not to travel by Lohit express and get involved for no reasons whatsoever. I boarded the train and was sitting next to a window and was lost in my world when another officer of my unit sitting next to me asked if there was any latest news from home, He suggested me to go to the STD booth nearby and make a call and find out soon since I will not be able to know thereafter once the train starts to move. I credited him for his noble suggestion and made a call. The officer sitting at the window watching my expression could make out from the happiness that the baby is in the world now. I returned back to the compartment and hugged the officer and gave him good news of the birth of my "little princess". I in my weirdest dreams will never be able to express the next 36 hours spent by me. They were even worse than the Commando course I did. I was feeling so handicapped of not being close to my wife and new born baby at this hour.

I reached Saharanpur and rushed to the hospital straight where Reena was admitted. I gave her a hug and thanked a million stars to have gifted me a girl child. Then I saw the little girl lying next to her with eyes closed but her hands in motion. It was mesmerizing to see my little girl, holding my index finger with her whole palm and giving me shivers all over. That connect of a father and daughter commenced that very moment. It was again a very pious day when my daughter was born as per Hindu traditions. It was "Karwachauth", the day when the married ladies fast the entire day praying for a long life for their husbands. I wanted to give her such a name that the word has names of both me and Reena. We finally thought of "Ridhima" (starts with Reena and ends with Madhur). My leave was about to get over and I reached my Unit back at Sibsagar. God had more in store for me and I received my posting orders to join "18 Assam Rifles". I learnt that the unit was presently close by and was about to move to a new destination. Next day itself I picked up my jeep and drove down to the battalion Headquarters of 18 Assam rifles and met the

Adjutant who happened to be my old friend. He gave me the input that the unit is moving to J & K and will be operating in valley under command of "RR" (Rashtriya Rifles). I met the CO who welcomed me to the battalion and extended all possible support I needed.

Returning back with positive vibes and awaiting my departure now. I was dined out by the fraternity of 20 Jat and having got my leave sanctioned by the CO of my new unit, I reported at Saharanpur and spent a few weeks of blissful togetherness with my family which was now complete.

"Always aim at complete harmony of thought and word and deed. Always aim at purifying your thoughts and everything will be well."

– Mahatma Gandhi

Chapter X

Sentinels of North East: The Assam Rifles

It's a distant dream for any *"Green Beret"* to have a continued happy family togetherness for long. Similarly, those beautiful moments with my wife Reena, Son Madhav, Ridhima (my new born doll) and folks, was so short lived that for the first time I ever felt the pinch of separation. Though with a strong but heavy heart, I moved ahead like a true Infantryman with the echo of words ringing in my ears. "You are not to question why, but only to do and die".

It was Oct 1994 and the chill factor had intensified. I reached Jammu railway station where I was received by the representatives of my new unit, "18 Assam Rifles". The typical blue coloured gypsy jeep picked me up and we reached "Dhansal" just adjacent to Katra, the base for the pilgrimage of Mata Vaishno Devi. I looked towards the cave temple on Trikuta Mountain, bowed and prayed, thereafter, entered the Unit location. To discuss further about an Assam Rifles battalion and my action packed tenure, it is imperative to learn about Assam Rifles as an organization.

Assam Rifles is the oldest paramilitary force of India as it was raised in 1835 called "Cachar Levy" as a militia force to aid the British Army in the hills of NE India. Today, it is 46-battalion strong outfit and is involved heavily in counter-insurgency operations in the North East. Although led completely by officers of the Indian Army, Assam

Rifles does not come under the MoD (Ministry of Defence) but the MHA (Ministry of Home Affairs). The Indian Army officers are on deputation with Assam Rifles during the duration of their tenure. Despite problems with equipment and training, the contribution of this force in opening the region to administration and commerce was nevertheless quite significant and over time they have become known as the "right arm of the civil and left arm of the military" in the region. The Indian government has also assigned the Assam Rifles its own Director General ex-Army of the rank of a Lieutenant General. A Tug of War for Assam Rifles involving dual control under MoD for operations and MHA for administration has been in news now and then. This issue, pending for a long time, however, the ex-servicemen of AR desires to place the AR under complete control of Army.

The role of AR has been phenomenal since pre and post-independence. Prior to 1965, this force was under the Ministry of External Affairs who were looking after NEFA affairs. It was transferred to the Ministry of Home Affairs when the latter took over this responsibility. The role of the Assam Rifles continued to evolve when in 1950 a devastating earthquake hit the Assam region and the force was called in to assist in the reconstruction of the areas and help in the resettlement and rehabilitation of those affected by it. Later the force was once again called to undertake a combat role when, during the 1962 Sino-Indian War elements were used to delay the advancing Chinese forces so that the Indian Army could establish its defence lines. During this time and since then, the Assam Rifles also maintained their peacekeeping role in the northern areas of India in the face of growing tribal unrest and insurgency. In this environment the maintenance of law and order, countering insurgency and reassuring the people of the region became important tasks for the security forces and initially they fell to the Assam Rifles before the Army assumed control, and then later their experience and goodwill in the region was drawn upon in order to assist the army in conducting these tasks. In recognition of the unit's skill in counter insurgency operations, three battalions were deployed on Operation Pawan in Sri Lanka between December 1988 and February 1990. Later in mid-1990's, six units of Assam Rifles were directed to J & K state to tackle terrorism whereas six RR (Rashtriya Rifles) battalions came to North east on a mutual exchange basis between both operational commands.

It was based on the highlighted concept mentioned above that my new unit "18 Assam Rifles" had moved from North east to J&K to participate in anti-terrorist operations along with the regular units of Army and RR battalions. The unit camped at Dhansal for nearly two months during which all personnel had to undergo pre induction training prior to induction for counter terrorist operations in Kashmir Valley. The duration at Dhansal was very interesting apart from routine training activities I learnt a lot about the work culture in a unit. The environment of an AR battalion is very informal and there is more than one way of doing a given task which really amazed me. It was unlike the way Army functions. One evening while taking a walk with officers after dinner, we were looking at the lights of Mata Vaishno Devi temple. Suddenly, an officer said, "let's walk up to the temple, pay respects and return back for our Physical training class before 0600hrs". It sounded quite unlikely to me but didn't revoke since everyone was in agreement. The Gypsy vehicle left us at Katra from where we started our climb. Situated in a cave in the Trikuta Mountain, the Vaishno Devi temple is one of the most popular pilgrimages in India. Perched at an altitude of 5200 feet, it involves a trek of nearly 12 km from the base camp at Katra. The climb of Vishno Devi Yatra itself is on a well-paved path with a gentle slope. Its duration varies according to the weather, the crowds and your speed. The route is dotted with shops selling souvenirs and devotional music, with pleasant views all along. You also have the option of climbing up stairs, which are shorter but much steeper and hence, more physically demanding. Despite this arduous journey, it is estimated that the shrine gets over one crore visitors annually, and more so during the Navratras (Indian festival of nine goddesses). We were on full steam ahead and took the gentle slope and reached the shrine in dot 2 hrs and 30 mins. Entered the cave and prayed at the Idol of Goddess for our safety and prosperity ahead in Valley encounters. While coming down we thought of taking a shorter route and came down by stairs in just about 1 hr and 30 mins. We reached the Camp location at 0330hrs while we still had comfortable two hrs of sleep. When we woke up it was suicidal….. All three of us who went for "darshan" had bad cramps however we still joined for our morning Physical training parade.

During the training itself we encountered one very hilarious incident. The dog training squad was present to give a demonstration of different types of dogs they train to include, sniffer, tracker, bomb disposal type etc. Just to give a background that in AR battalions we have troops mainly from North east hill tribes such as Mizos, Naga, Manipuris etc. After the dog show, one Naga soldier approached the in charge of the dog squad and said something but I could see him talking to him. The reaction of the JCO in charge of dog squad was indeed frightening. He just ran towards me to say something. I was worried as to what unparliamentarily language our boy had used to communicate? The JCO in charge said, *"Sahib, kindly permit us to leave just now"*. I told him, "under the prevailing situation it is not recommended to leave in dark, therefore you can leave in the morning but what has transpired between you and our jawan? And why are you so tense?" He replied that, *"Sir, your jawan was asking me to sell the dog to him to whom I said the dog is army property and cannot be sold. Still I asked him as to why does he want that dog"*? He said, *"Sir, the jawan said that, your dog has good amount of meat and I love eating dogs being from Nagaland"*. *"Sir, I got furious and scared therefore I wanted to leave before I get Court Martial for losing an army dog"*.

Our pre induction training got over and we were now seasoned enough to deal with the foreign and local terrorists in Kashmir valley. I would like to take a break to acquaint the readers with the genesis of the problem of insurgency in Kashmir which has been continuing since 1988 onwards. This issue is now globally talked about at all international forums therefore it becomes imperative to know about it. After independence from British rule, India and Pakistan fought a war over the princely state of Kashmir. Towards the end of the conflict, India controlled its most valuable parts, while there were sporadic incidents of violence but there was no organized insurgency movement. Jammu and Kashmir, a breeding ground of separatist ambitions, has been haunted by the insurgency since 1989. Pakistan played a vital role in converting it into a fully developed insurgency. More specifically, roots of insurgency were tied to a dispute over local autonomy. In July 1988, a series of demonstrations, strikes and attacks on the Indian government began the Kashmir insurgency, which during the 1990s escalated into the most important internal security issue in India. Pakistan claims to be giving its "moral and diplomatic" support to the separatist movement. Over six months, more than a hundred officials were killed to paralyze government's administrative and intelligence apparatus. The daughter of the interior affairs minister, Mufti Mohammad Sayeed was kidnapped in December and four terrorists had to be released for her release. This event led to mass celebrations all over the valley. CM, Farooq Abdullah resigned in January after the appointment of Jagmohan Malhotra as the Governor of Jammu and Kashmir. In this incident the underground militant movement was transformed into a mass struggle. To curb the situation AFSPA (Armed Forces Special Powers Act) was imposed on Kashmir in September 1990 to suppress the insurgency by giving armed forces the powers to kill and arrest without warrant to maintain public order. During this time the dominant tactic involved killing of a prominent figure in a public gathering to push forces into action and the public prevented them from capturing these insurgents. This sprouting of sympathizers in Kashmir led to the hard-line approach of Indian army. In 2015, former President of Pakistan Pervez Musharraf admitted that Pakistan had supported and trained insurgent groups in the 1990s. India has repeatedly called Pakistan to end its "cross-border terrorism" in Kashmir. Several new militant groups with radical Islamic views emerged and changed the ideological emphasis of the movement to Islamic. This had happened partly due to a large number of Islamic "Jihadi" fighters (mujahadeen) who had entered the Kashmir valley following the end of the Soviet-Afghan War in the 1980s. The Indian army has conducted various operations to control and eliminate insurgency in the region such as "Operation Sarp Vinash" in which a multi-battalion offensive was launched against terrorists from groups like Lashkar-e-Taiba, Harkat-ul-Jihad-e-Islami, al-Badr and Jaish-e-Mohammad who had been constructing shelters in the Pir Panjal region of Jammu and Kashmir over several years. The subsequent operations led to the death of over 60 terrorists and uncovered the largest network of militant hideouts in the history of insurgency in Jammu and Kashmir covering 100 square kilometers. This so called Insurgency or fundamentalist uprising took a sharp turn into terrorism.

The battalion was placed under the orbat of a RR Force Headquarter and immediately under a RR sector in general area of Kulgam tehsil in Anantnag district which was the birth place of HM "Hizbul Mujahidin", a dreaded terrorist outfit operating from Pakistan. It was winters and snowfall had started, I was commanding "E" Company located at Amnu village adjacent to Kulgam town. My Sector Headquarter was at proper Kulgam with a Brigadier posted there however my battalion Headquarter was almost 45 mins driving distance away. I have seen photographs of "Saifulla, then Deputy supreme commander of HM" taking salute of a parade of Kashmiri terrorists with arms at Kulgam High School on 14 Aug 1994, which was just 3 mins drive from my camp site.

The modus operandi of terrorists have always been to give an initial dirty wound by inflicting casualties to security forces denying time to settle down at a new place and demotivate them at the outset. I was fully charged up and awaiting such an action. My strategy to deal with them was to beat them at their own game plan. I had a bullet proof gypsy and had a selected team of five boys with me (including the driver). We six had a great connect of gestures and radio operating procedure. One day I was travelling in my area, when my driver heard some noise and said, "Sahab, IED (Improvised explosive device) has burst somewhere however it appears to be a weak one". I was surprised to hear him. He stopped the vehicle and all of us jumped out of the gypsy and spread in different directions. It was a site to see. Just behind the gypsy at the middle of the road, we saw smoke coming out of a small crater. It was actually an IED blast but as luck would have it, the terrorist who packed the IED was not an expert. The IED HE (High Explosive) got wet in the snow sleet and got diffused. Rather than blasting, it caught fire and started to burn. I and all my 5 boys were saved or else we would have been hanging on some tree in tatters. Thanks to Mata Vaishno Devi!! It was a lesson for me and a bigger lesson for the terrorists and the sympathizers around. The same night we laid two ambushes in that general area and saw some suspicious movement in the field close to a house which we had doubted earlier. Once the two guys got into the hut, we moved from our ambush site and cordoned it stealthily and summoned them to open the door or we fire. Soon enough there was a burst of fire from inside on us for which we were already prepared and under cover, on orders the LMG (Light machine gun) operator opened up with a long burst supported by two of us with our AK 47 burst fire. In no time both the terrorists were neutralised.

I informed the Sector Headquarters at Kulgam who immediately despatched the police party for the needful. Most importantly, I called the villagers and made them pick up the dead bodies of both terrorists and told them to move towards the road and near the crater created by the IED blast where the police van was stationed for loading and further disposal. It was just a part of psychological warfare to connect the dead terrorist and the IED crater while the scene was witnessed by the entire village and hidden terrorists too. My policy of *"Terror beats Terror"* and *"Zero tolerance to beat terror crime"* was understood by the villagers around. I was congratulated by my CO and the Sector Commander subsequently. Within a span of one year at Kulgam, I had neutralized a large number of listed terrorists in my area of responsibility. My Sector Commander used to call me, *"My Commando"*. During my tenure at Kulgam, another major achievement that I would like to share with my readers is that, on orders from my higher HQs, I was instrumental in creating a counter terrorist group namely, Ikwan- ul- Musalmeen at South Kashmir out of surrendered JKLF terrorists (A similar force already existed in North Kashmir). One of its sections was at Khannabal Sector and the other at Kulgam Sector. We trained and operated with them together and neutralized many terrorists both during covert and overt ops. The IUM created their own space and accommodated themselves separately in a proper camp site akin to that of army. The year 1995 gave Headquarters Victor Force and more so Headquarters 3 Sector RR with record neutralization of terrorists and capture of weapons/ war like stores.

I was asked by many if I was cited for an award to which my reply was...... *"Narrating a true action story isn't easy. What is told is, naturally, presented in the best light, the 20/20 vision of hindsight. What is unbearable, but sometimes equally heroic, is often never revealed. One has to strike a balance between what happened and what seemed to happen. There is the inherent drama, but also the confusion, not just of the 'dust and smoke' of battle"*. With respect to my statement above, I like to narrate two incidents which still pinch me even after my retirement. Firstly, I was in the midst of a fire fight with two terrorists in a village and one was already knocked down. The other terrorist was still strong and countering all our moves. Since I was in radio communication with my CO as well as the Sector Headquarters, I found my neighboring Company Commander with his QRT entering the operational site. He was probably dispatched by the CO in haste to beef up my operational strength. He along with his boys took positions when a "hand grenade" was popped up by the terrorist blasted off and a splinter got into the forehead of this officer. He was told to immediately get evacuated from the site and report to the Military Hospital at Srinagar. It was later learnt that the officer was neither admitted nor operated but registered as a battle casualty due to the splinter embedded in the forehead. The operation was completed once the second terrorist was eliminated in the fire fight and we returned back to unit. Next morning was very interesting to read that the Officer who got the splinter was reflected as officer in charge of the entire operation and recommended for a Shaurya Chakra, which he later received in actual reality. I thought maybe because of the injury he was considered for the award and avoided any questioning further. Secondly, I conducted a short raid operation with precision resulting in elimination of a terrorist in a village adjacent to Kulgam. I left the dead terrorist in location and informed the Sector Headquarters to notify the police. I was told to leave back to camp and they would get the formalities completed. Next morning it was so hilarious to read the situation report where, the staff officer of the Sector HQ was referred to have gone for the operation climbing a water pipe at night all alone and reaching the first floor further getting into a hand to hand fight with the terrorist ultimately killing him. The officer was later awarded a Sena Medal for Gallantry.

It was quite some time that I had spoken to my wife and parents. The nearest STD booth to make a trunk call was at Srinagar; I informed my CO about my move to Srinagar and would be back by afternoon. He gave me a task to interact with the Assistant magistrate at Pampore en-route to Srinagar and apprise him to meet the CO since he was a member in one of the Board of Officers with him and had to sign the proceedings. Now, this incident was very interesting and brings out the true character of a nonfunctional appointment still enjoying the power within disturbed Kashmir. I stopped my Gypsy and instructed my buddy to go in and inform that I would like to meet the magistrate. The buddy returned back with an assuming face and said, *"Sir, he says that he is a magistrate and he does not get up from his chair"*. I looked at my buddy and said, *"Give him respect then"*. The buddy understood and ran inside along with one more jawan from the Gypsy. Suddenly I found the so called magistrate came running out to my vehicle and started complaining that, *"Your jawans are misbehaving and were lifting me along with the chair"*. This was the time to counsel the self-esteem of the magistrate. I told him, *"Mr Magistrate, if you feel so strong about your portfolio then you must be aware that maintaining good governance and law and order in the state is also your responsibility. If you had done it right then probably I would not have been present in your state today. I just came to inform you that my CO wants you in the Battalion headquarters to sign the Board of Officers proceedings, kindly do so by evening today. Good day"*. I then proceeded to Srinagar and had a hearty talk to my folks and wife. By 5.00 Pm I was back in my Company Post. As I had thought correctly, my CO as well as my sector commander called me up separately later evening and asked if I had a pow wow with the magistrate at Pampore today. I narrated the story and all I got was a *"Shabash"* (appreciation).

My main purpose of making a call home as mentioned above was to apprise them that I was earmarked to attend a pre staff course at Palampur for duration of 3 months and the families were permitted to join. It was a big treat to be together and this time my kids would also join me. Palampur is an important city located in Kangra Valley. It is a famous hill station and was once a part of the Jalandhar kingdom. The town came into being when Dr. Jameson, Superintendent of Botanical Gardens, introduced the tea bush from Almora in 1849. The bush thrived and so did the town which became a focus of the European tea estate owners with an exception of the famous (former) Wah Tea Estate which was owned by Nawab Muhammad Hayat Khan and his descendants, until 1947. Since then, the Kangra tea of Palampur has been known internationally. Palampur is connected by the narrow gauge Kangra Valley Railway, Pathankot to Joginder Nagar. The railway station is named Palampur (Himachal). It is situated at Maranda, 4 km from bus stand.

The day arrived when I was across Pir Panjal ranges in an environment where I was not moving under the shadow of my buddy with gun or under the threat of a terrorist. I reached Pathankot railway station and that is the day when Reena along with Madhav and Ridhima were to arrive by train from Saharanpur. It was a family homecoming and smiles across all four faces exhibited happiness. My doll, Ridhima had started to walk and run and had the famous fountain shaped small ponytail on her head. We boarded the narrow gauge toy train which was a treat to travel in. The entire route was mystic and mesmerizing. The ideal weather conditions made it even more romantic. The train halted at Palampur and we hired a taxi to our earmarked allotted accommodation. Fortunately we carried most of the items including curtains since they gave us basic furniture with beds and mattresses. Days passed and I got busy in my studies whereas Reena and other ladies would join up and go out for a visit to various tourist spots at Palampur. She was even cooking at home only. I recollect, the Brigade headquarters organizing this course had arranged for a special bus for all of us participants to see the area around in Himachal Pradesh especially in Kangra Valley. It was a long trip where we visited Dharamshala, Mcleod Gunj, Jwala Devi temple, Baijnath and the tea gardens. All good things come to an end and so did this wonderful trip of my family at Palampur. I had taken a short leave to drop them home and returned back to Kulgam only to learn another good news that my second round of posting within Assam Rifles was out and I was to report at Zakhama (Nagaland) on my new appointment as Joint Assistant Director (Personal) in IGAR Headquarters (North). My new place of posting was a peace station with reasonably ok accommodation. Therefore, Reena was tasked to carry out packing of household luggage by the time I reach Saharanpur and we could dispatch the stuff by a small truck and rest travel by train till Dimapur (Nagaland).

It was again a long journey but nothing new for us. We reached Dimapur and were received by the representatives of my office. A car was available which ferried us all the way to Zakhama. We crossed Kohima en-route. I found Col Rishikesh Moitra of my parent unit, 20 Jat also posted there. We settled much sooner than we thought and it was an easy going life though. We could visit many places around and once a week we used to visit Kohima market to buy vegetables. I recollect a very interesting episode at the Kohima market, Reena and self were walking through the market when Reena saw a big basket full of puppies making noise and jumping around. She was a dog enthusiast and said, *"How cute puppies, but why are they in this market"*? I said, *"You might as well buy your vegetables first and I'll let you know on our return"*. She was not amused by my statement, however, she did her shopping and we returned. On the way back I told her the fact that the locals relish dog meat here in Nagaland. I looked at her and she was reflecting mixed feelings, her eyes were wet in love for the pet and wanted to puke too. We had a nice truncated tenure of just 6 months at Zakhama maybe we had something more shocking in store for us in our next tenure which was at Bareilly.

Chapter XI

The Tragedy: Bareilly

This was our first proper posting after marriage where I arrived as a complete family. Not considering Zakhama really, since it was a short and truncated 6 months tenure. Bareilly is a good blend of advancement, liveliness and peace. The city has exceptionally good education system with a number of good schools. People are relaxed and the madness of a metro has not caught on to it as yet. It has a good train network to major cities. It lies in the center of state capital and in proximity to national capital that has its perks in terms of transportation and business. It has its fair share of all the 6 seasons of the north. Summers are intense and very uncomfortable but winters are welcomed and celebrated. We were fortunate that we still have access to fresh vegetables and fruits and not adulterated or frozen food in spite of a huge population. Bareilly was not new for me since I commenced my journey in Army from here as a singleton, however, I am back now as a foursome.

Whenever I would meet anyone outside Bareilly, at first instance the song *"Bareilly ke bazar mei jhumka gira re....."* is remembered and further the question continues as to what is the background to it?? Well the answer to this question is a small incident (as I learnt from my jeweller friend, resident of Bareilly) that took place long ago ... The incident was about Teji Bachchan (mother of actor Amitabh Bachchan). One day a team of Bollywood (actor and actress along with a music director) visited "Bareilly ka bazar". At that time the music director was planning for a song for his new upcoming film... And during this visit the "jhumka" of "Teji Bachchan " fell from her ear and the music director noticed this event and related it like this (jhumka gira re bareilly ke bazar me)!!! He got the starting lines for his new song. He then decided to make a song over this event. Rest is history.

We were allotted a nice and spacious three BHK apartment with an outhouse for our maid. Well settled and the usual routine of a married family had gained momentum. Madhav was in class I in Army public school while Ridhima had joined a play school. Both schools were within the cantonment limits. However, my official setup had a large jurisdiction to include a vast operational area which was unique to this type of an organization. Nevertheless, all good hill stations were within our orbat and not to forget Saharanpur, my home station thereby moving along with my General for conducting Administrative inspections of Major installations and Regimental Centre's kept me amused and busy. Reena had made a few good friends and kept herself busy. Soon enough she picked up a job as nursery school teacher and was happy enough to pass her time and earn her own pocket money. A new addition came into our family..... my first car.... *A cherry red Maruti Suzuki 800(AC)!!* I drove the car all the way from Jalandhar to Bareilly via Saharanpur (Night Halt). Once I reached the house, happiness was the only emotion glowing from the face of Reena as well as the two kids. She did the honors of performing the rituals and the car was washed and then parked inside the garage. Subsequently it was a regular treat to take the car out on some pretext or the other.

Madhav was exhibiting signs of lack in mental growth however he was a smart child physically. His MRI of the brain revealed some flaws in lack of oxygen during delivery time which resulted in death of a group of brain cells. Reena was worse hit and the setback drew her even closer to Madhav. We visited a few neurologists and Madhav was diagnosed with mild *"Autism"* and a separate dedicated curriculum was planned for him. Reena took the challenge and dedicated herself to him and ensured not to send Madhav to any handicapped/spastic school. When he would return back from school, Reena would feed him lunch and take him to Rohilkand University on a pre-arranged appointment with a speech therapist to improve his speech. Similarly, lot of effort of improvement was made on him in other interacting skills as well. Subsequently, my parents also arrived at Bareilly and we started to live and enjoy a real pleasurable life which so far was just a dream. We had a few bridge players amongst colleagues in my office complex. Dad and I would get hooked on every Sunday and holiday.

My parent unit was in Udhampur and had received its move orders to Sikkim. The entire unit was at Jammu awaiting Rolling stock. When the train was placed and loaded, there appeared to be some issue on the Power (engine) connecting the train. Kashmir valley was hot again and the delay at the railway siding was causing a big trouble for the unit to think adversely. I was at Ranikhet at that point of time when I received a call from Reena stating that, *"Captain Raja Pillai just called up and said, Ma'am, kindly speak to your dad and help us out or we are going back to Valley"*. I just told her, you have no options but to speak to papa (my father-in-law). She did so and a couple of hours later, Raja called back that the engine has arrived and joined up with the rolling stock and they would be moving shortly, He further added that the special train will make a halt at Bareilly on the second morning from the start. Since I was at Ranikhet with the General, hence it was not possible for me to arrive but Reena had all the plans to visit them at the railway station. She got up early morning on that day of arrival of special train and packed breakfast for all officer families and milk for young kids. Both Madhav and Ridhima were fast asleep, she let the maid (who stayed in the outhouse) supervise the kids while she was away to the railway station. The entire 20 Jat fraternity was more than thrilled to find her at the station and thanked her for the sumptuous dishes she had prepared for them. As per Reena, it was a memorable get together which I missed immensely.

Soon a major civil military liaison conference was to be organized and the responsibility was entrusted to our headquarters. The conference was at state level and of the magnitude that the Chief Minister of UP, Central Army Commander and the Chief Secretary, UP State would be attending. Such event management was part of my portfolio and the venue for the conference was selected as *"Nainital"*. The conference was three months away and I had lot of plans up my sleeve. Initially I took a short trip to Nainital for two days and identified the venue for conference and accommodation status for all invitees. Having done so, necessary modifications in the infrastructure and procurement of stores for the event had to be catered for. I returned back to Bareilly and discussed with my superiors and got approval for the actions ahead. Once the ball went rolling then I decided to shift my office one month prior to the conference at Nainital holiday home. This time Reena too joined me for about a fortnight since the kids too had a long break.

Commonly known as the *"Lake District of India"*, Nainital is one of the most beautiful hill stations in North India. Surrounded by mountains on three sides Nainital is located around the beautiful lake "Naini". This lake resort is situated at a height of 1,938 meters. There are many legends associated with the place. According to one, Nainital has derived its name from the Goddess Naina while the other legend says that when the Goddess Sati lost her eyes, she was being carried by Lord Shiva and a lake was formed. ('Naina' means eyes and 'Tal' means lake.) Nainital is referred in the 'Manas Khand' of the 'Skanda Purana' as the Tri-Rishi-Sarovar, the lake of the three sages, Atri, Pulastya and Pulaha who were reputed to have arrived here on pilgrimage and penitence. Finding no water to quench their thirst dug a hole and siphoned water into it from the sacred Mansarovar Lake in Tibet.

The conference was just two day away and the day for arrival of all invitees commenced. It was a two day event and somehow gave me a feel as if I was organizing the UN Nations General Assembly where in the heads of the states would be making a speech. Apart from arrangements I was thickly involved in the briefing of my General during the course of the conference where his presentation on power point was also prepared by me. Irrespective of the stress I could handle all my portfolios well and finally got appreciations in open forum from all and sundry. I was the last to leave after ensuring a detailed inventory check and proper handing over to the officer in charge of holiday home. On my return back to Bareilly I took a week's leave to relax and spend some quality time with my family. The "millennium" was the buzz word those days and every one was planning a big deal for 31 Dec 1999 opening up to new "millennium 2000". We were enthusiastic too but had no major plans due to my official commitments. We planned to have a few good parties and have a big bash that night at Bareilly Club along with our colleagues.

It was Nov end of 1999 and Reena would often report to me pain in her low back, initially it was the home remedies of applying some pain gel and or a pain killer but that didn't work so I took her to the surgical specialist at the Military Hospital. The specialist got the X-Ray done and all was in place. He told her a few exercises to perform and gave a few pain killers and said, she would be ok in a weeks' time. However, that too didn't work and she was then referred to a gynecologist keeping in view the issue having a connect with the usual ladies problem. An Ultrasound was done but again all was considered ok. Reena was herself confused as to what it was since no other indication surfaced. On 04 Dec 1999 we had visited

Army School to attend parent teachers meet and also to receive the half yearly report card of Madhav. We were delighted to see a gross improvement in Madhav's performance and he had scored a good grade in spite of his medical issue. In fact his performance was much better than the students who were absolutely medically and mentally fit. We proceeded to the market and bought some ice cream which we all had while watching a movie "*Dil Se*" at home. We slept almost at midnight.

At 0300 hrs on 05 Dec 1999, Reena woke me up complaining of same low back ache. I gave her a rub of Voveron gel and said, it would get ok, sleep now. She woke me up again at 0400 hrs for the same problem. This time I woke up my dad and he recommended giving her a "Voveron SR" (pain killer) which the doctor had earlier recommended to take in case of shooting pain. At about 0500 hrs I woke up noticing Reena frequently visiting the wash room and vomiting. She didn't look comfortable at all and was repeatedly mentioning the pain. I called up the Duty medical officer at the Military Hospital, he happened to be the surgical specialist and well known to me. He said that at times the strong pain killer gives nausea therefore give her an anti-acid tablet and she should be ok, or else get her to the hospital. We waited for some improvement after administering the medicine but no relief in pain however the nausea sensation was better. I decided to take her to the hospital. It was a Sunday and a holiday at office and school too. I quickly changed into my track suit and was combing my hair while I heard a vague gargling sound erupting from Reena's throat. I just dropped my comb and ran to her and shouted for everyone. Dad, Mom and the maid came running inside the room and found Reena lying still with no response what so ever. I gave her mouth to mouth respiration, thumped her chest but would not respond. She was getting cold and blue. We were scared and stressed like hell. We used to live on the first floor and to get her down was to be thought of. I placed her on a chair and self along with the maid got her down, immediately got the car out of the garage and made her lie down in the rear seat with maid sitting next to her and my mom on the front seat. The military hospital was just 5 mins drive and I took the car till the entrance against the rule. She was placed on the stretcher and taken for emergency care while we all waited in the DMOs office.

Another 15 mins, the medical specialist was there and he carried out all her tests along with ECG. We were intimated that Reena was "*BID*" (Brought in Dead).

This was unacceptable and unbelievable!! It took some time for all of us to face the reality. The news had gone viral within the army fraternity and everyone within the cantonment arrived at the hospital being a Sunday. My mom was with the ladies discussing the past few days of activities where as my colleagues were trying their level best to console me. I was shattered and couldn't think ahead. That was the time my mom came and said that dad was alone at home with both kids and she must go back home along with the maid so the kids are looked after. I nodded and thereafter I was surrounded with officers trying to inquire as well as pacify. The Commandant of Military hospital who was also present, recommended that since it's a case of BID, it's better to rule out any foul play which inadvertently someone may play later, therefore we must opt for a post mortem through police at our level only. They needed my consent but like a zombie I just nodded to what all was referred to me. Her mortal remains were then moved out of the hospital and carried to the morgue from where they were to proceed to the civil hospital for post mortem. Everyone returned back and I too came home and found a large gathering already present there.

Honestly speaking, on returning back home it never came to my mind as if Reena is no more in this world however the grieving visitors kept reminding me, my kids and my parents about her absence. We were in an illusion as if she would be back soon. Madhav and Ridhima were too small to understand such a loss but they would start crying the moment anyone would meet them and hold them close. My mother is a strong lady and she understood her task allotted by God Almighty at such a crucial juncture. She got even closer to both the kids but this time not like a grandma but like a mother. Both the kids got fully absorbed in her love and affection so much that it became easy to handle them thereafter. Irrespective, we were still not out of shock till we finally carried out the last rites. The entire Bareilly Cantonment officers and ladies were present for the funeral. My in-laws, my sister and brother-in-law with both their boys, many close relatives from Delhi and Saharanpur and a young officer from 20 Jat(who was en route to YOs course) joined in. The post mortem report also arrived prior to the funeral which read "Death caused due to Myocardial Ischemia and presence of a large clot traced in the inferior side of the heart".

All rituals as per Hindu Jain traditions were fulfilled and the visitors from outstation returned back. My sister and in-laws stayed for a couple of days more then they returned back too. Now, the emotional void and emptiness was setting in. It became difficult to exist and I would weep when alone since I couldn't do so in presence of my kids and parents. I was forced to start going to work so that I would shift my focus a bit and stay stabilized and avoid negative thoughts. I would go to work and it would seem that everything was the same as it had always been until someone came to convey their condolences. But then I would come home just walking into that empty house. Reena was not there to say hello or ask me how I got on that day. Mom would be waiting for me with lunch laid on the table ... and most of the time I didn't eat it ... because I was missing what I had lost ... not just my wife, but also the person who used to look after me. That was when it hit me hardest. The feeling of being deeply known and accepted, the private jokes and references and language accrued over decades, the quotidian of my routine, the shared memories that now are mine alone to carry. She was not only my wife. She was also the one who would tell me if my socks matched; if my tie was straight, or if my hair was combed. She was able to tell me with one look if I was talking too much or saying something stupid. She was the one who would remember all the birthdays and special occasions, and all I had to do was sign and dispatch cards. She was good at all the things I am not good at. So she complemented me and made me more whole. God, I miss her so much. I feel like part of me is missing. A common theme among people who have lost their spouse is the debilitating effects of feeling entirely alone and incomplete. The sense of feeling like you have lost an essential part of yourself is both painful and disconcerting. The world suddenly looks like a different place, often odd and distanced. You are not sure how to cope with life in general, and sometimes you may even wonder if you even want to try.

I was reading an article which highlighted; "Grief resembles depression, if a person experienced the symptoms of depression in the first two months after a loss, the diagnosis would be "bereavement." But if those symptoms persisted past two months, the diagnosis would switch to "depression." This "bereavement exclusion" no longer exists, partly because of the timeline" Are people really supposed to be "done" grieving after two months? Can't grief last six months or a year—or, in some form or another, an entire lifetime? It's okay if you can't imagine any of this yet. What will help in the meantime is doing something about your solitude. It sounds as if you have a history of drinking, so you probably know that people tend to use substances in response to an emotional void, an emptiness that calls out for something to fill it. Connection is a different—and far more effective—way to fill that emptiness. Reena's absence had left a crater-sized hole, and anything I would do to create moments of connection—whether seeing a grief counselor, visiting a neighbor, sharing a meal with a friend, joining a group related to an interest or hobby, calling on people in my community (religious, spiritual, professional) for company, focusing on doing things that feel personally fulfilling or meaningful—would begin to plug the hole. The point was to engage, little by little—toggling unsteadily between my past and my future. I would never, ever stop missing Reena, but somewhere inside me I knew that reaching out to the living would help. My mother was a big motivating factor to show me light ahead and my kids barely 6 and 3 yrs would look into my wet eyes for some answer to which they themselves never asked a question. I took a vow to continue with full steam ahead and not look back for the sake of my children. I will do everything what my late wife had in dream store for both Madhav and Ridhima.

It was end December 1999; I had taken a long leave since it was winter holidays for my children too. Self, Parents and kids drove down to Saharanpur in my "Cherry red" (as Reena would call it often) via Haridwar where I along with Madhav came up to "Har ki pauri" for immersion of Reena's ashes into holy mother Ganges finally. That was the last I felt the physical presence of my late wife Reena. We reached Saharanpur by evening and we had very many visitors of our residential colony coming over to convey their shock and condolences. No one could ever think of a 31 year old physically fit lady would just kick the bucket so soon. Now the thought sneaking into my mind was my tenure at Bareilly about to get over and I was expecting my posting back to my battalion 20 Jat which was at Sikkim. Under the prevailing circumstances I couldn't have taken my kids along with me and similarly leaving them with my aged parents would also be incorrect without any help. Therefore, on our return back to Bareilly, the first thing I requested my General was to help me in getting a posting to my home town on extreme compassionate grounds. The General did so without even a question coming from him and referred my case with strong recommendations to post me at Saharanpur even if the rule needs an amendment. I received my posting to "Saharanpur" as "Administrative officer into a NCC battalion" just walking distance from my house. It was April 2000, I got all my household stuff packed up and hired a truck to dispatch it to Saharanpur while we all would drive back home in our car.

I recollect those words spoken on my dining out speech at the officer's mess of Headquarters UP Area, "I came to Bareilly as a joyful foursome but returning back as a shattered threesome"

My tenure at Saharanpur was a new mould for me and my kids. I got full assistance from my new Unit. However I was generally found in a pensive mood carrying out introspection about my future in Army. The present state does not permit me to carry on since I will not be showered all the charity during all my postings irrespective if even I give an adverse career certificate. In all probabilities my next posting would be in a field station and that too an operational one. My parents, relatives and close associates were dwelling upon me to stabilize my life once again so that the young kids get a mother and I can continue to serve in Army rather than running pillar to post in a corporate world. Such thoughts were not even in my distant dreams at that point of time and I would just shoot such ideas. Time is a big healer and I left everything on God Almighty to steer me to a logical conclusion if needed. My dad's friend approached him one day and discussed with him along with a few more friends together. Dad spoke to me and Mom in the evening about the widowed daughter of his friend and recommended for an alliance with me. As it was destined, the necessary rituals were over and Shikha came into my life after Reena. It will be incorrect for me to discuss any form of comparison; hence I'll leave it at this and rev up my journey further for which I had taken a vow never to look back ever.

Chapter XII

The Cutting Edge: 34 Rashtriya Rifles

My life had now accepted the shift and the pace. All of us at home were used to a new normal but the vacuum created still existed. I had firmed up to continue my Army service and took up a case voluntarily with Military Secretary's branch for my reversion back to active service. The case was acknowledged very swiftly and I received my posting orders to 34 Rashtriya Rifles (JAT). I was to report by end January 2002 in Badgam District of Kashmir Valley. I was fully prepared and delighted to go back to my favorite battle ground since I had earlier served in Kulgam with 18 Assam Rifles and had organized an anti-terrorist group at that time. I also had the experience of organizing an intelligence network and conducted umpteen successful operations in the valley. This tenure was RR specific therefore I would like to acquaint my readers about this wonderful organization before I go ahead with my terrorist hunting spree.

The RR (Rashtriya Rifles) as an organization was raised in 1990 by then Army chief Gen V N Sharma with Lt Gen P C Monkotia as its first Director-General. Initially, there were six such battalions, three in J&K and three in Punjab. Later, all the RR battalions were moved to Jammu and Kashmir as the valley got entangled in a gory conflict with Pakistan-trained militants creating havoc in the region. With the motto, *"Dridhta aur Virta"* (Resolute and Bravery) the force comprised of 65 battalions divided into five Force Headquarters —

Romeo Force, Delta Force, Victor Force, Kilo and Uniform Force. The Rashtriya Rifles being the star of the Indian Defense services as the largest counter insurgency force in the world organizes its battalion manpower strength with half of it coming from a specific Indian Army's Infantry Regiment, and the other half from the rest of the Indian Army. In an attempt to ensure that India's LoC (Line of Control) Divisions could perform their jobs i.e. engaging Pakistan, unhindered by guerilla action, the RR could carry out search operations, conduct crackdowns, raid suspected hideouts of militants, make arrests and seize weapons. The RR are themselves equipped with advanced weaponry, aircraft and other defense gear but the classic AK-47 remains their weapon of choice. The RR also has an exclusive network of local sources that are placed within militant organizations to provide ground-level intelligence. It is true that the original goal of the battalion is to be at the forefront in counter-insurgency operations and eliminate terroristic activities; however, it simultaneously assists in grass root development and winning over the hearts and minds by carrying out 'Sadbhavana' or Goodwill activities. The Rashtriya Rifles also undertakes a heterogeneous civic action program, intended at raising the standard of living, social, education and cultural betterment of the masses, implementing vocational education to youngsters, assuring their general empowerment, aiding to the education of women and a host of such people-centric initiatives.

I reported at the transit camp Srinagar, from where I was picked up in a *"Casspir vehicle"* (Bullet proof Infantry combat vehicle) and reached the Battalion Headquarters location at Beerwah (Tehsil headquarter) part of Badgam District of Kashmir valley. Initially I took over the command of "A" Company located at Beerwah High ground itself since I was earmarked to be the second-in-command once the present incumbent gets posted out. My stepping in the unit brought cheers as we neutralized two terrorists within a week and I was physically present in the operation. The CO was well versed with my anti terrorists skills which were unique and result oriented. He would let me plan operations hereafter and the intelligence set up established at the battalion headquarters was also refurbished and a daily record of terrorist movement was plotted based on "DFs" (Direction finders) and the transmission received from captured militant radio sets. We had almost accurate information of terrorist movement within the Area of responsibility of "Kilo" and "Victor" Force.

I had two of my favorite battle hardy teams namely "Ghatak (Commando) Platoon" and secondly "Second in command QRT" (Quick Reaction team). My special operations to include search and destroy missions in the valley were conducted with the support of these two teams only. In my previous tenure I had identified all towns, villages, and terrain features as existing in the entire South Kashmir whereas this tenure gave me a complete exposure to the Central Kashmir. I enjoyed physically visiting the *Gullies* (passes) on the mighty Pir Panjal Ranges on foot and appreciated the routes that the militants would take to enter Kashmir valley from POK (Pakistan occupied Kashmir). Now, fully settled, brushed up with the terrain and information on terrorists……. I commenced planning and executing operations with full steam ahead. "Mosque" is a holy place of worship for Muslim community. However, it was seen with experience in the valley that these terrorists would invariably misuse these holy shrines and take refuge whenever they get cornered by forces thinking that Army would not dare enter the mosque or damage it resulting in a free passage to them later. 34 RR (Jat) has to its credit "three mosque operations" where in five terrorists were neutralised however no damage was caused to the religious place. I was physically present in all the three operations as Officer in charge and also motivated surrender of a terrorist with weapon. In fact my first such operation was in March 2002 itself at Village "Radbug" close by where in one terrorist was eliminated with recovery of an AK 47 Rifle.

Notwithstanding the operational scenario in valley, the cohesiveness and camaraderie amongst the RR fraternity was enjoyed to a great extent. I remember whenever we would leave for operations generally later part of the night and reach our destination....... We had to establish a proper cordon in dark so as to ensure no civilian leaves the cordoned area and if they do were checked and summoned before opening fire. Spending the entire night fully awake and ensuring nothing untoward happens and thereafter carrying out a crackdown of the village early morning to congregate the entire village persons at a central place like a school. Thereafter, organizing detailed search of the village for presence of any terrorists inside. Let me first explain the term "Crackdown". Once the village is cordoned at night, it is understood by the villagers that the village would be searched in the morning. The representatives of RR outfit would call for "*Mukkadam*" (village headman). He would be interrogated by the Officer in charge of Operation and questioned if any terrorist is in hiding in the village, if yes, then he can be alerted to surrender and his life would be saved or else during search if any terrorist opens fire or is cornered then he would be eliminated. After that, the Mukkadam would go to the Mosque and make announcement through PA (Public address) system and all villagers would congregate at a given place as identified. The ladies and kids would sit at a place while the male members at a different place. I recollect a very funny incident here, my buddy noted that I was standing for past many long hours and he spoke something to the Mukkadam, later a young man arrived with a chair and kept it close to me. I thanked and asked the man, "What does he do"? He said, "I am the chairman". I was taken aback and asked him again, "Chairman of which Company or agency"?? He said, "No sir, who so ever is responsible to get the chair for the officer in charge of operation is called chairman". We all laughed for a while. Subsequently, once the search parties culminated there detailed search and all was found correct, a clearance form is given to the Mukkadam to sign that the forces have not carried out any atrocities or theft in the village. Once the documentation is over and the villages are satisfied, the search parties return back.

Varied instances of plucking and enjoying fresh juicy apples from an apple orchard, roasting fresh sweet maize for breakfast can never be forgotten. Whenever there was a major operation involving many sub units, all of us would carry our packed breakfast/lunch or dinner as per meal timings. When the right time approached and we would congregate for a meal that was a treat to watch……. All tiffin's would come under command the second in command, that's me!! Some would be containing roasted chicken, chicken curry, mutton, fish curry, aloo paratha, scrambled eggs, Poorie aloo and even Maggie noodles. Thereafter, it reminded me of the famous scene of Bollywood film *"Satte pe Satta"* where Amitabh Bachchan, the eldest brother, would give a war cry and everyone would just bash on regardless. None of us knew each other before but the camaraderie was phenomenal.

We had a real soldier as our general at Headquarters Victor force; He had a lot of trust in me for my way of functioning in such an environment. I was the only second in command to attend his conferences since I was loaded with information of areas concerning central and south Kashmir. He would invariably land at battalion headquarters whenever I had a successful operation and present me a bottle of Scotch whiskey. One day I was away on a special mission with hard intelligence to get a foreign terrorist "Bilal Habshi". The timing somehow was not correct but the information was, the terrorist escaped firing at one of my boys who sustained a GSW (Gun Shot

Wound) in his leg. I was sad and in no time I got a call from the General saying, *"Madhur, not to worry, but get Bilal soon. How much time do you give him more to live"*? I was on a thinking mode but I replied, *"24 hours, Sir"*. He said, *"I will wait, good luck"* and he hung up. Now it was a prestige issue and I sat in my "Radio room" hearing to all militant conversation and getting deciphered by the "JaK LI" boys posted with me. Finally I got the hint and kept it as a secret till the eleventh hour and at mid night hit the same village and raided a couple of houses I was suspicious on. Bilal was there and he opened up with a heavy volume of fire so as to put our heads down and can manage an escape again. We were prepared for it and there was a fierce fire fight for a few minutes which eventually resulted in silencing him. At the break of Dawn, we cautiously searched the hut and finally got "Bilal Habshi" lying in front of me in a pool of blood. The General was more than pleased with this action and praised me in open forum and as promised gave me a bottle of Scotch once again.

There is no dearth of Operations being carried out by forces all over the Kashmir Valley. I recollect the famous words of Late General Zia Ul Haq of Pakistan, "We understand that defeating India in a conventional warfare all by ourselves is very difficult. Therefore, we must design a battle scenario wherein Pakistan spends Re 1/- and India has to spend Rs 1000/-." This is how the concept of LIC (Low Intensity Conflict) came into being and since that day Pakistan is Hell-bent upon keeping the Kashmir pot boiling. Nevertheless, the Indian forces have been adamant enough in dealing with this menace and also through diplomatic channels ensuring that Kashmir is one and an integral part of Indian Republic.

During my tenure with 34 RR I personally led a number of successful operations as Company Commander, second-in-command and even as officiating CO which resulted in neutralization of 43 terrorists. However, I would like to give an account of a very meticulously planned and executed operation which resulted in elimination of ten hardcore terrorists (eight foreign and two locals) along with personal weapons and hoards of war like stores. This operation was so far was one of its types in the entire Northern Command which subsequently became a case study. "OPERATION VIKRAM" was conducted in October 2002 based on an intelligence input by own source and supported by DFs of terrorists. I discussed with my CO that a large group of foreign terrorists were planning an action at Budgam District Headquarters to destroy the ballot boxes post recently concluded elections. I led the Operation on 20 October 2002 with multiple CASO (cordon and search operations) of four villages with myself located at Village Mirpura. Shortly when the search commenced, the terrorists made an attempt to run away but were cornered by the cordon scouts of Village Mirpura. They got channelized into a water channel running between large vegetable gardens. I swiftly moved with my QRT (quick reaction team) and a fierce gun battle ensued. Sepoy Sarwan Kumar of my QRT rushed with his Light Machine Gun after the terrorists while firing it like a rifle from his hip position eliminated four terrorists one by one. He was severely wounded due to a GSW on his chest and was evacuated to Military Hospital Srinagar where he succumbed to his injuries. I along with my two boys got into the water Channel and crawled for a distance from where we could view the terrorists now hiding adjacent the wall of the water channel. A fire fight started once again and I eliminated two terrorists. By then the balance of them were also silenced by our team and the gun fire stopped completely. On detailed search we witnessed the operation resulted in elimination of ten hardcore terrorists out of which eight were foreigners and two locals. Nine AK- 47 Rifles, two pistols and much war like stores to include hand grenades, Rifle grenades, ammunition all types, radio sets, daggers etc were recovered. We lost Sep Sarwan Kumar Dhukiya (Parent Unit 15 JAT) who later was honoured with a KIRTI CHAKRA (posthumous), SHAURYA CHAKRA to Hav Rajbir Singh, SENA MEDAL for Gallantry to Maj Madhur Goyal and 2 x COAS Commendation Cards to Nb Sub Khilona & Hav Bijender Singh. In addition we received complimentary messages from the entire fraternity including the Army Commander, Corps Commander and Gen Khanna our Colonel of Jat Regiment to only name a few. This Operation was an excellent case study of a large size operation with correct information, analysis and planning, need based modification during the conduct without any confusion and 100% result.

The Commanding officer was away at Srinagar on some official purpose when this Operation was launched. On termination of Operation, we all returned back to our base and as a ritual all of us got together and made a big war cry and stayed in silence for 3 minutes in respect of late Sarwan kumar who laid down his life in the highest tradition of Army. Loss of Sarwan was a major setback to us but this is the price we army guys pay while guarding our nation and maintaining the sanctity of our national borders or fight against the anti-national elements within. Subsequently, it was learnt that the Corps Commander, Force Commander were about to land and the Sector Commander had already reached our location. I briefed the Corps Commander about the entire plan and execution of this operation while I saw the CO had also reached the base by now. The Corps Commander continued hearing my briefing and later congratulated each and every one of us who participated in the operation. By evening all outstation visitors had returned back and the vacuum created by Sarwan in my QRT was being felt a great deal. We all visited the temple available in our headquarters location and prayed for him. There was a change of Guard and the CO had received his posting orders while a new one was posted in.

It was 14 Aug 2003; I was taking a walk around the helipad with our new CO and in general giving him a brief of things around.

Suddenly I found the Adjutant, Maj AK Bensala, running towards us with a big smile and some news hidden in his belly which he just threw up reaching us. He informed that the Honors and Awards list has been de classified for 15 Aug 2003 and our unit 34 RR (JAT) has got a quiver full of awards. He also mentioned to CO that, Maj Madhur Goyal, second in command has been awarded with a Sena Medal for Gallantry. It was a great feeling and I rushed to the temple and paid my respects and thanked God Almighty, Subsequently, I made a call home and furnished this good news to my parents, sister and my wife. I received an official message to be present for Investiture ceremony at Mamun Cantonment on the Army Day ie; 15 Jan 2004.

It was "Army Day", the 15th day of January 2004,

During the Investiture Ceremony,

A citation was read out loud, and

A young Major stood silent in rapt attention

In front of the Army Commander and all silently listening....

The citation read………………..

"With utter disregard to his personal safety,

Major Madhur Goyal crawled through the water channel,

Approached towards the firing terrorists, and

Killed both of them in one to one fight.

The officer displayed exemplary courage and

For his act of valor, is awarded with

SENA MEDAL for GALLANTRY".

With his heart racing and chest filled with pride

And, under thunderous applause

Major Madhur Goyal *marched smartly to the Army Commander*

Who pinned the award on his Olive Green's

On behalf of the Hon'ble President of India.

Thereafter, **SENA MEDAL** *got affixed*

To Major Madhur Goyal's name as a Suffix

For the rest of his life.

The hunting spree continue thereafter till I received my posting orders in October 2004 to report at Chandigarh and take over command of "1452 Pioneer Unit" close to the Airport location within "N" Area Complex. All good things come to an end and I bid farewell to Kashmir Valley hale and hearty with the blessings of God Almighty and ending my tenure fully satisfied. Looking ahead for a happy family get together at Chandigarh once again.

Chapter XIII

The Chandigarh Chapter

"Upon returning, the bloody, wounded warrior needs only but laugh at the spotless, armchair critic."

– Criss Jam

At times when I try to drape myself with a self-lining of life, I perceive a familiarity of own self with loneliness which occasionally makes me feel that I as a soldier can also survive without love or poetry since I am used to leading this hard life!!!! The tenure in valley was a satiating one which gave me honors and awards as well as mental satisfaction for having done justice to the nation when called for. It was a great send off from 34 RR (Jat) and I took an Army courier flight in the massive "IL 76" Transport aircraft of Indian Air Force which landed at Chandigarh in Sept 2004. Since I was on preparatory leave, I dropped my luggage with the new unit and boarded a bus straight to Saharanpur. It was a Sunday and on reaching home, the delightful smiles on everyone's faces brought the much needed warmth in me. We were all in a *"Sab Chandigarh chalo"* (Let's all go to Chandigarh) mode, however, the academic session of kids was the hindrance. As it is, I was to initially apply for a house and Chandigarh being a high pressure station, allotment of entitled accommodation takes some time. We finally decided that final shifting with family would unfold by end March 2005, by then all issues would have been settled.

Chandigarh, as the capital of Punjab and Haryana, and by itself the Union Territory is a prestigious city. The face of modern India, Chandigarh, is the manifestation of a dream that Pandit Jawahar Lal Nehru envisaged and Le Corbusier executed. Picturesquely located at the foothills of Shivaliks, it is known as one of the best experiments in urban planning and modern architecture in the twentieth century in India and a quality of life, which is unparalleled. Chandigarh derives its name from the temple of "Chandi Mandir" located in the vicinity of the site selected for the city. The deity 'Chandi', the goddess of power and a fort of 'garh' lying beyond the temple gave the city its name "Chandigarh". Serenity and a city are two diametrically opposite concepts, which however, get belied in this 'City Beautiful'. Chandigarh is a rare epitome of modernization co-existing with nature's preservation. It is here that the trees and plants are as much a part of the construction plans as the buildings and the roads. India's first planned city is a rich, prosperous, spic and span, green city rightly called "THE CITY BEAUTIFUL". Keeping in view the need for the investment of investible surplus, the city administration has taken a number of major initiatives to upgrade the infrastructure in Chandigarh, to boost economic growth in the region. Chandigarh is emerging as a regional hub in the areas of service industry, education, health, information technology, food and vegetable processing etc. Chandigarh's economy is changing in character as the knowledge revolution sweeps the country. This gateway to Punjab, Haryana and Himachal Pradesh is now a tri-city, flanked on the Punjab side by Mohali, a budding metropolis that boasts a world-class cricket stadium, an international airport and luxurious high-rises. And on the Haryana (and Himachal) side, there's the growing city of Panchkula.

It was a wise decision since the initial few months emerged to be very taxing and the role as commanding "1452 Pioneers Unit" at "N" Area Chandigarh was a major responsibility too. My immediate Headquarters was at Leh and I had to make a few visits there to settle earlier issues. Getting on to the brass talks, my unit had an important logistics role to perform, somewhat akin to "Packers and Movers". We were responsible to pack fresh and dry food items, other consumables goods, oil and lubricants provided by the ASC (Army Supply Corps) in IAF transport aircrafts on skid boards and prepare them in air drop loads for difficult areas of Siachin glacier and other snow bound inaccessible mountainous region of HAA (High Altitude areas). Now I understood how we got our food stuff while operating at such great heights of Central Glacier. This entire action used to commence early morning @0300hrs onwards at the airfield and the first flight would invariably take off by 0600hrs. The troops then returned back to unit by 0800h and have their breakfast and rest. Our work timings were totally incoherent to the regular workers. However, our office timings would remain the same and I used to go to office as per standard working schedule. Initially, I would often visit the airfield early morning while the boys were at work and I had also made friends with numerous IAF officers flying these aircrafts on daily sorties. One day one of my known IAF Pilot invited me to fly along with him on an air drop sortie in Northern Glacier and have a first-hand view of how the air drop takes place from an IAF perspective. I welcomed the invitation and next early morning at 0500hrs I was all decked up in my uniform, reached the airfield. My name was manifested in the flight roster as an observer and we took off sharp at 0600hrs. The flight was a 2 hr 45 mins sortie and I loved the early morning aerial view of Chandigarh starting from the lakes and gardens to the foot hills of "Shivalik" which grew bigger into mighty Himalayas and finally all fully clad with snow.

AN-32 is a light multipurpose transport aircraft designed to maneuver day and night in tropical as well as mountainous regions. It features advanced cargo handling devices and a cargo door fitted with a ramp to ease the loading or unloading of freight. It is also incorporated with an upper cargo handling device to load and unload 3,000kg of payload. The packed cargoes are placed on the pallet by a demountable roller. Semi-automated locks fitted in the roller equipment detach the pallets and decrease the aircraft's idle time. Now, the Pilot indicated me the DZ (Dropping Zone) on ground which was a flat area beginning with "T" mark made by drums and covered with orange parachutes to stand out in snow. However, it was still difficult for me to sight them. The Pilot commenced the descent and both the pilot and navigator got on aircraft oxygen while I along with the flight engineer and the two pioneer jawans got on portable oxygen. The flight engineer positioned himself at the tail of the aircraft on one side of the load with headsets to communicate with the crew whereas the army jawans were at the rear of the load towards the cockpit. All were secured to the aircraft by belts. The aircraft was de-pressurized so that the ramp could be opened and aircraft prepared for drop. After that the ramp was slid open below the belly of the aircraft, the load was already tied up to the skid boards with parachutes on top and the whole contraption was on rails. During descend when the nose was down, the mechanical locks were removed and now the electrical locks were the only thing keeping the load from moving out of the aircraft. The aircraft was maneuvered to the correct line of drop on a slight descent so as to keep the load in front and not resting on electrical locks. Now it was a matter of accuracy as the aircraft had to be at the correct height, speed and direction at the point of drop. At the precise time, the navigator started the time of 5-4-3-2-1 and switched on an amber light in the rear of aircraft indicating everyone to be alert. The electrical locks were simultaneously released and switched on to green light. The pilot put the thrust lever fully forward and raised the pitch altitude to a nose high while in coordination the two jawans gave a push to start the load rolling and the flight engineer called out load rolling, load out. The parachutes were tied to the aircraft with lanyards. When the load was clear of the aircraft, they pulled the parachutes to deploy clear of the aircraft and the navigator closes the ramp and the pilots begin a slow climb back to base. The aircraft is re-pressurized and reheated and oxygen masks removed. I took a sigh of relief and moved into the cockpit conveying my gratitude to the IAF brethren who have always been up and about to assist the ground forces.

I was in mean while allotted a good ground floor accommodation keeping in view of my parents' ease and safe movement. Above all I was also promoted to the rank of "Lt Col" (Lieutenant Colonel). The family kept moving up and down from Saharanpur to Chandigarh and back but the moment final exam of kids materialized, I got them all at Chandigarh permanently. Both the kids got admission in "Bhawan Vidyalaya", a co-ed school. We took a week to settle and the usual household chores took the lead. I, my mom and dad have always been great admirer of flowers, not only just appreciative but maintaining a garden was our hobby too. My allotted house at Chandigarh within "N" Area had a vast open space on all three sides. Thanks to all our previous occupants who had planted a few good flowering as well as fruit bearing trees earlier. The morning ritual early summer was to spring out of bed and rush to the garden. The "Amaltas" in the garden would be in full bloom and the breeze would be showering the tree's delicate golden petals all over and beyond. Madhav and Ridhima would bathe in the gentle fall with outstretched arms and an upturned face. Then, there was the blazing saffron of "Gulmohars", Roses of six different shades and the mauve of "Kachnars" in our main garden. We all fell in love with the city too soon. In fact I won the best garden competition prize twice during my stay. Our vegetable garden had 18 different varieties of vegetables that were difficult to consume. My wife would send a basket full twice a week to my unit cookhouse for the benefit of jawans. Initially all of us were regular visitors of Sukhna Lake, a perennial lake flanked by the majestic Himalayan foothills, gorgeous Zakir Hussain Rose Garden, with its astounding varieties of roses, the Bougainvillea Garden, with its profusion of colours, and Shanti Kunj for the quiet it offers, with its gently trickling stream and undulated terrain. But the most unique and fascinating of them all is Nek Chand's Rock Garden, a wonderland of more than 2,000 sculptures built entirely out of industrial and home waste, laid out in mosaic courtyards linked by gorges and human-made waterfalls. The shopping, entertainment and business area in Sector 17 was the heart of the city which has now progressed to the Elante Mall in Chandigarh's Industrial Area (Phase I).

It was Jan 2005, one evening my parents were on a routine walk when my dad complained of some discomfort in his chest and also reported of mild pain. I took him to the Section Hospital within "N" Area complex and the doctor carried out his ECG. He was not too happy about it and said that it's better to refer him to a Cardiologist for further investigation. We were all tense; however I planned to take him along next day to Command Hospital. My dad was detected with CVD (Cardio vascular disease) at the Command Hospital, Chandimandir. The Cardiologist was a very jovial personality and was on temporary attachment from R&R Hospital Delhi Cantt. On carrying out detailed scrutiny of dad's heart, he said, "Uncle you might need a single graft or an angioplasty, just don't worry". He even advised me to get my dad to Delhi soonest so that we get the Angiography done for which he provided me with a reference note so I don't face any issue on reaching the R & R Hospital. The appointment was fixed for the next day of reaching Delhi and Dad was admitted the very day. The Angiography brought out the need of a "CABG" (Coronary Artery Bypass Graft) for single artery which was 90% blocked. He advised us to take a decision soon for the surgical procedure and do not let dad undertake any stress till then.

We finally decided to get him operated at "Apollo Hospital" since the best cardiovascular surgeon was available with them. My wife along with the kids was at Saharanpur while self and mother came to Delhi and stayed with my sister. When dad was admitted at Apollo Hospital, that evening was we were all tense and just keeping our fingers crossed. The surgical procedure commenced at 0600hrs next day and I was the first person to get permission to visit him in the ICCU where I found him on a mobile stretcher post-surgery attached to numerous tubes and valves. He could recognize me and showed thumbs up. The Chief surgeon was also present who confirmed that the surgery went off well. I returned to the waiting area in lobby where my mom was present and gave her the good news. We prayed and then had a nice cup of coffee. Subsequently, we had daily visitors once he was shifted to the room and on being discharged from the hospital; dad came to my sister's house to recoup while I returned back on duty. Later, on complete recovery the entire family joined back at Chandigarh.

By now I got the hang of my new job and I wanted to do my bit as a leader to provide welfare measures to my boys who had been working day and night for the welfare of the troops in contact with such adverse situations of war, inhospitable terrain and inclement weather. I spoke to the Commander "N" Area who was my administrative superior for additional funds and resources which were granted. I judiciously utilized them and created worthwhile assets for troops. There living barracks were fitted with desert coolers and quality curtains. The bathrooms were provided with much better cleanliness and hygiene facilities. The cook house was provided with latest gadgets for quick meal preparation. Water storage facilities were also improved. I created an "IT skill centre" with three computer work stations and motivated the boys to generate interest in learning computers. A small gym with some important equipment and a hair dressing salon were also created. The troops were indeed happy about it and this motivated them to perform even better. This resulted in virtually "zero" disciplinary cases with full output and as a result, 1452 Pioneers was adjudged as the best pioneer unit amongst the total 16 of them. Sometimes later in 2006 was the award ceremony at Bangalore for which I was earmarked to go and collect the trophy.

The city beautiful attracted many family visitors to my habitat. My sister with family was one of the first to visit. They had a 5-6 days stay and we visited every possible tourist attractive site possible. We even visited Kasauli hills and Pinjore gardens one of the days. I recollect my nephew had appeared for his interview for "Accenture" and started his journey in corporate world from here. I bought my new car, "Ford Ikon 1.3 Flair (petrol)" and disposed of my Maruti 800(Cherry red) which I bought while at Bareilly. My new found hobby cum passion for "Money Markets" (Stock market) developed a great deal and I got involved in it. I would spend hours into it on learning skills during late evenings on my PC while everyone slept. Soon enough I opened my trading account with a broker in civil area and got on with the daily trading keeping a range bound capital with limits. It was a mixed result and I thought I could do even better and studied more on its technical issues. That bore good fruit and since then I've been following this passion with a smile. Not boasting, but I've even started to assist my close friends and relatives with updates and my analysis of the markets on daily basis. I have a good number of such friends who still fall back on me to take advice on "money markets" or their "investment portfolio".

Shikha, who joined the folds of Army fraternity in year 2000 as my wife, was absolutely ignorant to the world of Olive Greens. In fact the situation under which this alliance materialized, did not encourage me much to apprise her about the organization as such. Soon enough I was away to Valley with 34 RR and everything went in cold storage.

This was her first exposure to army culture and specially being the wife of an "OC" (Officer Commanding), she had many responsibilities attached to it and was aware of it. Her maturity helped her to get over it very soon. I am thankful to all the ladies of my parent unit, 20 Jat, and other friends who were present in Chandigarh at that point of time and helped her in grooming and adjusting to the army family. She got an exposure of dealing in ladies meet and welfares etc with their help. My tenure of 34 RR had already taught her the meaning of separation, the living alone, the single-parenting, the multi-tasking, the moves etc, one of the biggest challenge an army wife faces! And trust me it was more arduous than it actually sounds. The warmth of Army fraternity made her forget all the negatives of Army life very soon. We shared the common platform together at many instances at Chandigarh giving us a feel of blissful togetherness and to her a new entity. Since then there is no looking back and Shikha has not left any stone unturned to keep pace with my military nuances.

My elder nephew (Uday) was to get married and all of us were to reach Noida by end June 2006. My new Ford was all decked up to transport us for the big event. I recollect the appalling incident when all of us were travelling on the GT Road at good speed of 120 kmph when a white colored Maruti 800 car visible to me from a distance but suddenly came very close since it was at halt in the middle of the road. My dad on the Co-driver seat shouted to brake and did so………. alas!! It still banged the bottom of the little white soap case. I and dad were worried if no harm to the passengers inside the Maruti had taken place. To our surprise a lady driver and her daughter Co-driver opened the gates and came out shouting at the top of their voice and started to take pictures of our car and number plate along with my picture. There were a few exchanges of words but nothing untoward. My dad was very humble to accede to their requirement in spite of their fault. A police patrol arrived and we took our cars on to a side towards the "Dhabas" and started to discuss with the police. On introducing myself as a Lt Col and the other party ladies were also from Army back ground, the police didn't want to enter into the issue and said that, "Please resolve it mutually and avoid any legal complication". My dad paid two thousand to the lady towards the denting painting requirement of the boot and they left happily. The problem was with my car which had a fatal carburetor accident with all coolant drained out and a bent bonnet. The car was not in proper shape to go ahead. I called up Ford Service and their recovery van arrived from "Service Centre at Karnal" promptly and towed it back for repairs, in the mean time I had hired a Tata sumo to ferry all of us to Noida. We rejoiced the grand marriage of Uday for three days and on return once again we had to hire a car back to Chandigarh. My Ikon was delivered back to me at Chandigarh in same shape as good as new with no repair charges on me since everything was under insurance cover.

All good things come to an end and so did this wonderful tenure. I got a shock when I was told by my head clerk that a telegram has been received in respect to my posting stating that I have been posted to Headquarters 40 Mountain Brigade at Baisakhi, Arunachal Pradesh and the move is "Forthwith". In army parlance "Forthwith" movement stands for move to be undertaken within 24 hours. I was highly perturbed for the first time on my posting at such short notice and I had sincerely thought of taking up a stand this time with the Army Headquarters since my mother had to get her eye operated for IOL transplant. I had precisely completed 2 yrs at Chandigarh when my posting order was issued. I called up the Military Secretary's branch and spoke to the Officer in charge my section and apprised him of my present issues. He said, "You can send us in writing and we will analyze". It was not a satisfying answer to me since it is was a "Forthwith" posting, therefore, I requested him, "I do not have any problems on proceeding on posting to Baisakhi, but there are umpteen issues pending presently for which my physical presence is essential and I need time of about three months". The officer said, "Three months is not possible however, I can grant you EJT (Extended joining time) for 30 days". That was also working out since I had full 60 days annual leave balance for the year and would be able to fulfill my domestic responsibilities. Accordingly, I was officially posted out but was retaining the same accommodation till 31 Mar 2007 on academic grounds. I handed over the Command of 1452 pioneers to Col Kohli and continued residing at Chandigarh till I finally departed for Baisakhi. The only regret I had was that I could not do the honors of proceeding to Bangalore and receive the "Best unit competition Trophy" which was later received by the new Incumbent.

"Even if things don't unfold the way you expected, don't be disheartened or give up. One who continues to advance will win in the end."

– Daisaku Ikeda

CHAPTER XIV

THE HIMALAYAN LAND OF ORCHID & KIWI: ARUNACHAL CALLING

"The mountains are calling and I must go"
— John Muir

When the Sun first forays India, it glosses upon Arunachal's wild forests and ethnic communities. Arunachal, the "land of rising Sun" which is a rambling mountainous territory, a land of enormous rocks and dense forests, gentle streams and mocking torrents, presents a breath-taking display of nature in all her glory, raw and un spoilt and in wild abundance of flora and fauna, customs, language and dress. This diversity of topographical and climatic conditions has favored the growth of luxuriant forests which are home to myriad plant and animal forms adding beauty to the landscape. Living in this unbelievable cradle of nature are the colorful and lively tribes of Arunachal Pradesh for whom the forests and the wildlife are of special significance. I commenced my Journey towards the end of Dec 2006 from New Delhi to Guwahati by "Rajdhani Express". This super express with adequate luxury where you are fed every now and then leaves with you with only one regret of not sleeping well during the travel. I reported to the transit camp where I was received by an NCO and a jawan from the Brigade Camp who briefed me that further movement is permitted only with the convoy which is slated to move tomorrow early morning. I was tired and not hungry. Took a quick wash and just hit the bed only to wake up early at 0400hrs.

The convoy marched off from transit camp at 0600hrs and the route taken to our first night halt destination "Tenga" (Division Headquarters) was via > Gowripur > Baihata Chariali > Mangaldoi > Mission Chariali (Tezpur) > Balipara > "Bhalukhpong" (The border check post of Arunachal Pradesh where special permit/passes are checked for Non Arunachali civilians, however not applicable for Indian Armed Forces) > Tippi > Sersa > Nechifu > Tenga, thereafter, next morning would move in our own Brigade transport with a different convoy to the second destination, "Senge transit camp" where I would carry out seven days acclimatization procedure since present at the height greater than 9000 feet ASL. The route followed would be Tenga > Bomdila > Munna > Dirang > Sapper > Senge transit camp and then finally to my Brigade Headquarters location at "Baisakhi" which was at an altitude of 12000 feet ASL and needed second stage acclimatization. The entire route was full of scenic beauty and natural waterfalls with majority of water falling on the highway and I could see the convoy passing under it with most of us extending our arms out of the window to feel the chill of fresh mineral water. The entire area was surrounded by the Eastern Himalayas, dense forests and pristine rivers. West Kameng is a district of Arunachal Pradesh which shares an international border with Tibet in the north, Bhutan in the west, Tawang District in the northwest, and East Kameng district in the east. The southern border is shared with Sonitpur district and Darrang district of Assam. The name is derived from the Kameng River, a tributary of the Brahmaputra that flows through the district. Our Division Headquarter as well as the Brigade Headquarter has its main role in this much important district of Arunachal Pradesh. The topography of the district is mostly mountainous. A greater part of it falls within the higher mountain zone, consisting of a mass of tangled peaks and valleys. In West Kameng there are three principle mountain chains – part of Sela range, Bomdila range and Chaku range. The Sela range consists of a series of mountains arranged in the form of a big line from Tibet in the north to Bhutan in the west and thus forming a tough terrain to pass through. The altitude of Sela range varies from 14,000 to 15,000 feet and Sela pass is 13,714 feet high. The Bomdila range has an average height of 9000 feet. South of Bomdila range lays the Chaku range (foot-hills range) having hills of quite low altitudes and is full of tropical forests with trees of great economic value and various types of wild game. The inhabitants of the district comprises mainly of Monpa tribe. By and large the inhabitants are Buddhists though Akas, Khawas and Mijis believe in indigenous religion and follow partly Buddhist and Hindu practices. Every tribe has its own society and village council.

On reaching Tenga, I kept a surprise from my readers. My parent unit, 20 Jat, was presently located at Tenga and the CO was Col Jayesh Badola, my youngster once upon a time and a great friend too. He sent a gypsy to receive me at the transit camp and I was to stay for the night at my Battalion guest room and have some nice fun and frolic reminiscing our earlier joyful days in the unit. I doubt if I slept that night!! Jayesh and Self kept chatting and laughing the entire night when I realized that its late enough and I need to freshen up to move with the convoy. I had the luxury of having a light vehicle which picked me up at my guest room and later joined the convoy en-route thereby saving over one hour of early reporting. Let me apprise the readers about the strategic importance of Arunachal Pradesh/West Kameng District with respect to India as well as China. Arunachal is the remotest Northeast Indian state which shares a 1,030 km, unfenced border with China and undoubtedly occupies a space in China's South Asia strategy. China continues to proclaim that a vast stretch of almost 90,000 sq kms of Arunachal Pradesh belongs to it and to substantiate it, China had invaded parts of Arunachal Pradesh during 1962 conflict and since then India's border with southern Tibet remains disputed. This contributed to the 1962 Sino-Indian war that was waged mainly in Arunachal and resulted in a series of lessons learnt by India. Arunachal Pradesh no doubt provides strategic depth to India's Brahmaputra Valley and security to Bhutan on it entire eastern flank by geographical contiguity. Bhutan would then be in the claws of China from both its flanks if Tawang is given away. This would be detrimental to India's security. China's borders would then rest on the plains of Assam; India might as well write off its other North Eastern states. The Chinese obsession with the Tawang Region is totally strategic in its aims. In any future conflict with China and if India singly or in coalition with some other power develops offensive capabilities against China, this region offers the shortest cut to China proper and to Tibet. India's communications infrastructure in this region developed in World War II for US military aid to China is existent and can be further improved. Arunachal Pradesh therefore is of vital strategic importance for the territorial integrity and defense of India's North East states and is non-negotiable.

The state has remained "sensitive" from India's security perspective and even Indian citizens require special permission to visit it. This has severely hampered development, but the resulting isolation has not been entirely unwelcome to its prejudiced tribal inhabitants. The state is claimed by China and significant portions of its populace feel that India has kept the state intentionally underdeveloped for decades, preferring to use it as a buffer against Chinese aggression much like the British did during their Raj. India has left Arunachal Pradesh underdeveloped in the misguided hope of having the mountainous state serve as a natural, physical buffer against the Chinese. However, ethnically and geographically removed from mainland India, Arunachali's could be feeling some growing bonds with China as their awareness of greater development (and economic opportunity) across the border increases. Infrastructure was not developed because of the anxiety over possible Chinese intrusion into the state and so it is impossible to travel by road from east to west in the state. All east-west travel by road must go through neighboring Assam. The lack of infrastructure has in fact made access to the Chinese border very difficult from the Indian side, while the Chinese have built infrastructure to facilitate movement for their military and people.

Enroute to Senge transit camp we crossed Bomdila and Dirang. It would be incorrect not to speak about Dirang which is a place of immense scenic beauty and natural marvels; a must visit for anyone seeking bliss and quietude. This place has an idyllic location for a peaceful retreat up in the hills of the northeast with the snow-capped mountains, gushing streams and lush greenery for company. National Research Centre On Yak; a Centre responsible for conserving the Indian Yak is present here. Dirang Dzong, a tribal area on the shores of Dirang river is a must visit too. The architecture of this tribal colony is stunning; made of stone and wood, the houses here are over 500 years old. The Dzong Fort in particular is quite a marvel, with Buddhist architectural influences. Though it's in ruins now, they're proof of the architectural brilliance of the olden days. For those who love to sit by a Hot Water Spring, here's your chance. There's one in Dirang; it flows from the nearby hills, and into river Dirang. Rich in sulphur and known for its curative powers. Black-necked cranes migrate to Dirang valley from China during the winter months and make for quite a spectacle; and then fly back to their homes during April and May. Kiwi fruit and State orchid flower (Rynchostylis Retusa) are grown here in abundance due to ideal terrain and weather conditions available. Our Convoy stopped a little later at "Sapper

TCP" (Traffic check post) manned by the corps of military police, for breakfast break. I relished the sumptuous "Dosas and Idlis" (South indian dishes) here. This TCP was part of our own brigade Headquarters under Baisakhi. Subsequently, we reached Senge and I checked into one of the rooms earmarked for me since I would be here for next six days undergoing acclimatization.

The routine for acclimatization would start my day early with monitoring of my blood pressure, pulse, temperature, chest wheezing and SPO2 levels. Thereafter, I would go for only 500m walk on the first day which gradually increased every day along with going up the gradient too. I was found fit to move to higher reaches and finally left for Baisakhi which I was longing for past many days. The temperature at Baisakhi was subzero with no sunshine. I later learnt that Baisakhi is known to get a maximum of two months sunshine in the entire year if you are lucky. I can ratify the statement since I stayed for two complete years and found myself lucky too. My Brigade Commander was Brig P Satish and a thorough gentleman. I could get along well with him since he was a very pragmatic person and a great leader of men. There was one Infantry Battalion and an Artillery Regiment present at Baisakhi. We had a huge helipad and when the air traffic was quiet, we used to convert it into our cricket ground. We played many matches between the Brigade Headquarters and the Sikh Battalion present. Overall life at Baisakhi remained paralyzed due to heavy snowfall, no sunshine and extreme wind and chill factor. Staying indoors in offices or residence/officer's mess was the normal @Baisakhi.

Apart from operational role at the International border, our secondary role was the safe passage of convoys from Tenga to Tawang which used to be thrice a week either way. Standing outside my office I could get a clear glimpse of the ecstatic "Sela Pass" which we have read about in all war books depicting 1962 Sino-Indian war. The zig zag highway from Baisakhi to Sela with an increase in altitude of over 2000 feet looked gruesome to travel on in subzero temperature. The AQMG of our Brigade HQs whose job was to monitor the convoy movement would generally be away on various other commitments and Brig Satish would let me officiate in his place most of the time. It was a great experience but I did a good job and would never let down my Commander. The most buzzing joint at Baisakhi was the "STD booth". All officers JCOs and Jawans would reach the booth whenever free to connect with their families, friends and folks. I found that place to be very entertaining and invariably the caller would forget the place he actually is and would get totally engrossed in his domestic and regional linguistic vocabulary to convey his feelings across. All guys in waiting would never mind but cheer him up during his call home. Although they would part away when they found an officer making a call home and speaking to his wife specially.

Now that I was well acclimatized for second stage and could plan ahead to visit Sela Pass and beyond, I took permission from my Commander and planned a visit to Tawang and to higher reaches where we would be there if the balloon goes up. I was accompanied with a youngster, a Lieutenant from the Corps of Signals who was in charge of providing communication. We were in the same gypsy and reached Sela Pass and stopped for about an hour to speak to our boys braving the weather on daily basis at 14,500 feet. They felt motivated since they don't get people talking to them physically. There was a huge lake close to the pass which was frozen and reminded me of the famous Pangang Tso of Ladhak. Moving further, we reached "Jaswantgarh TCP". This place has a great sentimental value based on 1962 Operations. Jaswant Garh famously known as Jaswantgarh War Memorial and this memorial is in honor of late Rifleman Jaswant Singh Rawat. He was an Infantry Jawan from 4 Garhwal Rifles, and for his bravery who gave a bloody nose to the Chinese; Jaswant Rawat was honored by a memorial at the post where he fought the Chinese army. 17 and 18 November 1962 are two days enshrined boldly in India's abundant military heritage. These two dates, so close to each other, symbolize valor and sacrifice of the highest order; they relate to the Sino-Indian Border Conflict 1962. As the Chinese People's Liberation Army (PLA) fought a largely unprepared Indian Army, thrust into battle at forbidding heights in winter, post after post and defended area after another fell in the way of its advance. Almost a month after the Chinese launched their invasion on 20 October 1962 in NEFA and Ladakh gaining large tracts of territory and forcing the Indian Army to withdraw, two brave units fought an epic battle, each to bloody the Chinese and restore the image of the Indian Army. Coincidentally, one battle was in each of the two theatres of conflict - NEFA (now Arunachal Pradesh) and Ladakh. This war memorial is at an altitude of about 10,000 feet and an interesting feature is that it has a temple-like structure is dotted with the camouflage pattern all over the memorial. However, today you will find all the Garhwal Rifles deployed on the Indian western borders but an interesting fact about this memorial is that you can notice at least few personnel here, taking care of Jaswant Garh (Rawat). One can make a day out of it by simply visiting the attraction and snacking along with various quick foods like delicious "samosas and pakoras"(indian snacks) along with tea/coffee to keep you warm during cold weather.

We moved further to Tawang and stayed for a night there and also visited the location where the Chinese and Indian military have their peace talks/ Border management meet in event of any pow wow. Next morning we moved out of Tawang on a long drive to our operational area. We reached beyond 15000 feet and it was very chilly as well as dry. The cough was troubling me when one of the locals provided me with a bottle of "Rhododendron medicinal syrup". I had a table spoon full and I could feel a burning sensation in my food tract just akin to having neat Vodka. To my surprise I was feeling relieved of my cough which later cleared off after a few more intake of same medicine. We reached the destination and there was a snow hut available for our night stay. There was a Kero Bukhari inside the hut which was keeping it warm. We refreshed ourselves and had our dinner and lied down. The rarified atmosphere was initially making us difficult to breathe naturally but soon we got acclimatized since we were already operating at 12000 feet at Baisakhi. We could get some sleep but woke up to start a fresh day which was surprisingly sunny. It was a bonanza for all of us and we went on a long walk inspecting the entire area where ever our brigade HQs bunkers were there. We checked a few bunkers on the heights from where the war would be fought in the actual scenario, noted down all the points to brief the Commander on return.

We returned to Baisakhi the next day only to learn that we have to recreate the existing war memorial at "Nyukmadong" close to Sapper TCP. The memorial was in ruins and was not looked after either by the district administration or by the previous army units available. Our Brigade Commander took special interest in refurbishing it and arranged funds to do so which has indeed given a face lift to the War memorial. The Nyukmadong War Memorial is located on a spacious 1.5 acre plot of land, overlooking the famous battle ground of 18 Nov 1962. It nestles in a three tired terraced landscape with beautiful coniferous trees planted around. The main memorial is in the form of a 25 feet high 'Chorten' conforming to the local ethos and traditions. Entrance looks like a main access way, to a monastery, in typical Buddhist style. On both sides of the memorial, plaques listing the names of officers and Jawans, who died here on that fateful day, have been erected. The memorial is staffed by JCO's, who are more than willing to narrate detailed account of the battle. A visit to this memorial invariably turns in such a solemn occasion that every visitor leaves the place with a sad and heavy heart.

I was about to complete two years tenure at Baisakhi and as per stipulations, no one is permitted to stay beyond two years. I had also taken up a case with my section in Military Secretary's branch to post me closer home on compassionate grounds due to my dad not maintain good health. I was acknowledged by them and was posted to NCC (National Cadet Corps) which was a shift in the way of functioning and ideology for me hereafter. I knew that I would get minimum of two such postings in continuation and was happy for it. My reporting station was "Muzaffarnagar" which was just 59 km away from Saharanpur. I was given a warm send off to mitigate the chill effect and reached Guwahati from where I took a flight straight to Delhi to reach home earlier.

Chapter XV

Shift in Ideology: NCC Lifestyle

"Young men, my hope is in you. Will you respond to the call of your nation? Each one of you has a glorious future if you dare believe me. Have a tremendous faith in yourselves, like the faith I had when I was a child, and which I am working out now. Have that faith, each one of you, in yourself—that eternal power is lodged in every soul—and you will revive the whole of the country"

– Swami Vivekananda

It was Jan 2009 and I finally returned home exactly after 2 yrs and 2 months of gruesome tenure at Baisakhi. The dim sunshine of January at Saharanpur was far more comforting and warm than the brightest of sunshine witnessed during the entire tenure at Baisakhi. My dad along with Madhav was at the railway station with his car to receive me. I gave dad a deep hug and so did Madhav to his dad and we drove back home. Shikha was waiting at the main gate and Mom along with Ridhima were sitting next to the swing in the drive way. All faces conveyed pleasantries and compliments that I look fit and well-shaped however, mom as usual like a true mother remarked that I have thinned down, making everyone laugh on the statement. It was a great over whelming feeling meeting everyone together after so long. We all sat down and started to discuss further plans. The first question asked by my parents and Shikha, "Will you be residing at Saharanpur and move up and down to Muzaffarnagar or would you take up some adhoc accommodation there itself and visit only on weekends and holidays". I had both options open but the decision was not mine but the Group Commander who was my boss at Meerut.

Although I had a week's leave combined with the preparatory leave but I was informed that 82 UP Battalion NCC at Muzaffarnagar was undergoing its CATC (Combined annual training camp) and it would be good for me if I join earlier so I can understand the SOP (Standard operating procedure) of running a NCC camp on real time basis. I respected the idea and joined the camp site next day by driving down to Muzaffarnagar in my own car. I met the outgoing CO who was to hand over to me and fortunately the Group Commander was also paying his mandatory visit to the camp site. The entire environment was a bit depressing initially keeping in view my recent arrival from an Army Brigade Headquarters. Nevertheless, this was my new life and I had to settle with it. I earlier had a truncated exposure with 86 UP Battalion NCC at Saharanpur and was generally aware of the administrative handicaps of an NCC Battalion. The outgoing CO and I were discussing whole lot of issues including my personal need of residing at Saharanpur. He said not to worry and I can continue to stay at Saharanpur during the Camp duration and thereafter, as a CO you have to take your own decision in NCC. I understood and kept away from discussing this issue with the Group Commander. The Group Commander arrived and we all heard a briefing given by the CO, who was also the Camp Commandant. Lot of my cobwebs on conducting a camp got cleared after the briefing. We had lunch and the Group Commander returned to Meerut and so did I to Saharanpur. I gave the good news to Shikha and my folks that I would continue to reside at Saharanpur and proceed to Unit on regular basis. I got my monthly rail pass made which would entitle me to travel with ease and not get worked up driving on daily basis up and down. I will take some time to acquaint my readers with the genesis of NCC and the road ahead.

The Kashmir War of 1948 taught a very important lesson to India, that freedom needs to be protected by strong Armed Forces. Its immediate manifestation was that the recommendations of Kunzuru committee were placed before the Constituent Assembly (Legislature) in Mar 1948. The Central Govt accepted the opinion of the Provincial Govts and the Standing Committee's recommendations for the formation of a Cadet Corps which was to be named as "National Cadet Corps", as recommended by the Kunzuru Committee. The Bill received the assent of the Governor General on 16 Apr 1948, and the National Cadet Corps came into being by an Act of the Parliament Act No. XXXI of 1948 designated 'The National Cadet Corps Act 1948'. This Act with 13 clauses, prescribed the formation of the National Cadet Corps in India. The first step in the process of raising of the NCC was setting up of the NCC Secretariat now called Headquarters Directorate General NCC. In fact, even before the NCC Bill was passed by the Constituent Assembly (Legislative), the Ministry of Defence had set up the nucleus of the NCC Secretariat, with Col (later retired as Chief of Army Staff) Gopal Gurunath Bewoor as first Director of the NCC. He took over as Director of NCC on 31 Mar 1948. The NCC which has now 13 lakh cadets on its rolls, had started with 20,000 cadets in 1948. The 'Aims' of the NCC laid out in 1988 have stood the test of time and continue to meet the requirements expected of it in the current socio–economic scenario of the country. The NCC aims at developing character, comradeship, discipline, a secular outlook, the spirit of adventure and ideals of selfless service amongst young citizens. Further, it aims at creating a pool of organized, trained and motivated youth with leadership qualities in all walks of life, who will serve the Nation regardless of which career they choose. Needless to say, the NCC also provides an environment conducive to motivating young Indians to join the armed forces.

Institutional Training in the NCC is being conducted in the Colleges and Schools as the principal means of training to nurture core values enhance awareness and give exposure to basic military skills and knowledge. Emphasis is on practical training. Case studies, wherever possible is used to facilitate active participation and better assimilation. Examples from India's freedom struggle and wars fought by India, post-independence, also supplement relevant subjects to generate secular and patriotic fervor. The instructors and the cadets grasp the importance of this training and participate actively. The ANOs (Associate NCC Officers) are the regular teachers/professors in schools/ colleges who are enrolled in NCC as honorary ranked officers and are responsible for the discipline and conduct of their institution cadet outfit. The PI Staff (Permanent Instructor) staffs are the JCOs and NCOs of regular army posted with the NCC Battalions to impart training in physical fitness, Drill and military subjects including firing skills. Therefore an NCC Battalion has on its roll about 1500 cadets. I recollect the big board outside my NCC unit hanging had the following written on it…….

YOUNG MINDS OFTEN RUN WILD,

BUT NCC MAKES YOU WISE.

FROM A BOY TO A MAN,

YOUR JOURNEY WILL BE FULL OF LIFE.

DISCIPLINE AND HONOUR WILL LEAD YOU IN LIFE.

SPORTS, ADVENTURE, CULTURE, TRAVEL & EXCITEMENT,

IS OUR SOLE COMMITMENT.

COME AND SERVE THE NATION AS YOU LEAD,

BE IN NCC AND TAKE THE LEAD, WHERE YOUR ASPIRATION WILL MEET.

"NCC BECKONS YOU TO ALWAYS TAKE THE LEAD"

After taking over the reins of 82 UP Battalion NCC at Muzaffarnagar, my routine was fixed with dad dropping me in his car at the railway station at 0800hrs. I would board Utkal Express which would generally take 1hr to reach Muzaffarnagar, my office Maruti Van would be waiting to take me to office. Likewise my return was at 1400hrs and I would be back home by 1500hrs. It was a decent tie up and the family was in harmony. The CO in an NCC unit is mainly involved during Camps where he has a major role to play by ensuring safety, security and discipline of cadets apart from the accounting and management issues. Those 10 days camp makes the CO like a father of 600 boys and girl cadets or even more. The morning train journey of one hour was the most interesting part of my day's routine. The time was perfect, weather was conducive, and all passengers in good mood after a good night rest. An enormous load of daily passengers would board the train along with me to join their offices at Deoband, Muzaffarnagar, Meerut etc and they all had their favorite compartments to sit every morning in selected groups. Some would just sit and place their briefcase on the lap, get the pack of cards out and start playing "Sweep". Many would only discuss about some interesting incident of last evening or the typical constipated boss whereas some would explain the technique as to how he is getting his house painted. At times there were altercations too which were resolved by the other co passengers amicably. However, the return journey was not similar though, where everyone was hungry and jaded. They would neither play cards nor discuss anything bright. Just the frown on each forehead spoke volumes. Often I found all those hardy boys and chirpy girls of the morning trip resting their head on the neighbor's shoulder with their eyes winking in sleep often and on.

I recollect a Camp of Roorkee NCC Battalion was conducted at Saharanpur and I was detailed to proceed as an Administrative officer. The camp site was lodged within the premises of IPT-IIT Saharanpur (Institute of Paper Technology wing of Indian Institute of Technology, Roorkee) and maximum cadets were engineering under Grads of IIT Roorkee. However, near about 100 students were local boys and girls from Inter colleges of rural belt too. When those local cadets were placed in hostels with attached bathrooms they were bowled over by the generosity of the organisers. More so, taking bath under a shower was like a dream come true for them. The genuine and honest feelings were not hidden from their faces. The so called learned cadets of IIT initially laughed it out but adored them and made good friends with them consequently. Dealing with girl cadets was a difficult ball game. The instructor would inadvertently shout at the girl cadet as he would do so in routine with any boy cadet, this would immediately result in shedding tears by the girl cadet and watching her cry the gamut of other girls would start off wailing for no reason. The lady ANOs and the *GCI* (Girl Cadet Instructors) would then come to help and control the situation. Distribution of meals was another big issue. Boys would hog endless whereas the girls would get satiated with just two chapattis. Some wanted more salt and some less, same with sugar and spices etc. Invariably, the meal time was full of action and reporting.

It was Jan 2011 and my dad's health status suddenly started to deteriorate. He was 83 then. His heart was strong after the bypass surgery but his lungs were persistently under an asthmatic attack. He would get well with medication and at times had to be admitted in hospital too. It was late Feb while in hospital at Saharanpur; his condition worsened and had to be evacuated to a multispecialty hospital at Meerut. He was placed on NIV (Non Invasive Ventilation) initially, but had to be intubated soon. He did not show any improvement and signs of multi organ failure surfaced. He finally breathed his last on

03 Mar 2011. My jijaji, Sudhir Gupta, was with me at the hospital and we transported his mortal remains to our house at Saharanpur next early morning for the last rites. All relatives and friends were intimated and were present for the funeral. My Sister, Ruby, was with my mom consoling her at this juncture and Shikha was handling the house management. Both the kids were heart broken and especially my daughter, Ridhima, who was her Dadaji's favorite. She was busy with her class XIth exams during this period. Life at home had come to a standstill and I could feel tons of emptiness surrounding his loss.

We are never really ready to lose a loved one no matter how sick they are. While there are no tables given for how long grief should last for such a loss, I think it will take a while for the pain to subside. But time does seem to help lessen the pain. Many people I know ask "how my mom is doing", showing their concern for her. Rarely does anyone ask how I am doing. The loss of a father produces a complicated form of grief in a son. The emptiness created by a father's death quickly fills with volatile emotions — sadness mixed with relief, affection mixed with lingering resentments, appreciation mixed with sharp criticism. That's why a man's grief over his father's death often emerges in disguised forms. I haven't just felt one emotion since my father passed, my experience has been more like travelling the world. Each stage of your journey will be completely different, and as you wander through your grief, emotions will come and go. It's been nearly 10 years since my father died, so I think I can safely say I've been through it all; the shock, the sadness, the anger, the guilt, and, eventually, the acceptance. There's no universal manual to help you deal with the loss of a parent, so when it does happen, a lot of feelings, occurrences and interactions with other people can take you by surprise.

My responsibilities at home had gone up manifold and my main focus was to ensure mom is taken full care off. Shikha was by my side in doing so. I left no stone unturned to give priority to my mom for any decision being taken even if it does not concern her. It took three months by the time she was out of the shell and was looking ahead to participate in household responsibilities. She has always been a strong woman and her presence motivates me even now. Nevertheless, I had firmed up to quit my Army service since I couldn't leave mom at Saharanpur if I had to proceed on a field posting elsewhere and if I take her along then her health would not permit. She was happy only in her house at Saharanpur. I had prepared my documents and finally before taking a shot, I thought of informing her. She stopped me from taking such a step and told me to continue. Shikha was very generous at this stage and recommended that where ever I proceed on posting, she would be here with mom and take care of kids since both of them were in there crucial stage of academics. Ridhima was pursuing her class XII th and Madhav was doing his CA as well as appearing for BCom final exams. I appreciated Shikha's stand and discarded the decision of quitting as of now. I was about to complete three years at Muzaffarnagar and received my posting order to Udaipur as CO of 5 Rajasthan Girls battalion NCC at Udaipur, Rajasthan.

I was to leave for Udaipur in Dec end 2011, but prior to that we had a very important family event to witness. Udit, my younger nephew, was getting married to Pooja, girl from Oddisa and Udit's office colleague. It was a love marriage and we were thrilled to be party to the marriage proceedings with me as *"mama"* has to play an important role. Sudhir Jijaji arranged for air tickets of the entire *"Baraat"* from Delhi to Bhuwneshwar and back. Mom, Shikha, Madhav & Ridhima and self-accompanied the Baraat. I drove down from Saharanpur to Delhi in my Ford Ikon ensuring this time to respectably bypass all Maruti 800 cars en route. We as baraat had a wonderful flight with lot of plans in making during the flight. *'Mili'*, my elder nephew's wife was incharge of all such activities. She created some daily theme and involved everyone and also gave me and Shikha to dance on the song, *"Kajrare tere kale kale nain...."*. This was the first time I witnessed a wedding in Odissa culture and tradition. Once the local customs were performed thereafter we followed our customs and solemnized the matrimony. It was a great wedding and we returned back to Delhi with the *"Dulhan"* (Bride). I and family returned back to Saharanpur and was now gearing up to move for Udaipur. I was fortunate enough since my Course mate Col Arun parashar was also one of the CO's in the same NCC Group Headquarters at Udaipur but posted at Bhilwara while another friend of mine was posted as Administrative officer in the Group HQ who was once posted in NCC Saharanpur. I got adequate feedback from both of them and my arrangements were well catered for at Udaipur.

I chose to drive down from Saharanpur to Udaipur by road in my own car. It was a 950 Km long journey and I planned to do it in two days. The first halt I took at Gurgaon at my sister's house and next morning was a long drive of almost 700 Kms. The road was perfect and my Ikon just kept moving making pace with my thoughts. I bypassed Jaipur, Ajmer, Bhilwara and Chittorgarh. I deliberately mentioned bypassing these wonderful places to confirm that I was not on a tourist visa. Surprisingly, I reached Udaipur before sunset and was accommodated in the guest room of Group HQ officers mess. Honestly, the first thing I did was to go to the terrace and see the view of Udaipur at twilight, it was mesmerizing. The charm that Udaipur holds can be seen from the names that it has been bestowed with...... The City of Dawn, the City of Lakes and Venice of the East are just a few of the names with which Udaipur is often referred. Udaipur presents a historical spectacle which is sure to spellbind every visitor with its unequivocal architectural beauty and hypnotic cultural vibrancy. Located in the state of Rajasthan, on the southern side of the majestic Aravalli hills, this city attracts travellers from all over the world. Whether you are seeking a holiday with nature and scenic beauty or amidst the grandeur of ancient structures, whether you are looking for a break from monotony by indulging in some cultural colorfulness and pampering of palate with mouth-watering cuisines, Udaipur is the answer to all your holiday dreams. Historically the city of Udaipur was also the capital of Mewar Kingdom, after it was founded in 1553 by the Maharana Udai Singh II. The palaces, grand gardens, museums and cultural shows present a glimpse of its rich past, while lakes and surrounding hills soothes your soul and promise a refreshing stay.

I visited my new unit and took charge of my appointment as Commanding Officer. The New Year of 2012 was knocking the door and we were all invited by the Udaipur Brigade as an annual tradition for celebrating the New Year's Eve in their officer's mess which was on the banks of *"Lake Pichola"*. This lake is an artificial fresh water lake which was built in 1362 AD, and is impossible to miss when on an Udaipur visit. On this lake are located some of the most popular places to visit in Udaipur such as the islands of *Jag Niwas* (famous Lake Palace hotel) and Jagmandir. On the eastern bank of the lake stands the City Palace. A boat ride in the lake which offers an unforgettable view of the city is quite popular among visitors. I made sure of calling my wife Shikha on the countdown of 2012 and subsequently had a talk with my mom, Madhav and Ridhima too. It was late when we reached back our officers mess which was located on the hillock astride Lake Fateh sagar. Its again an artificial lake, named after Maharana Fateh Singh, Fateh Sagar Lake is located on the northern side of Lake Pichola to which it is connected through a canal. Surrounded by hills and woods, this lake makes for a delightful visit. In this lake stand the Nehru Island and a small islet consisting of Udaipur Solar Observatory, also known as Connaught Bundh. The circumference of this lake was 9.2 Km and was my favorite evening walk unhindered. I started to love this beautiful city of lakes.

My Battalion was a special one. It was the only Girls NCC Battalion in the Group HQs encompassing the entire jurisdiction as that of the complete Group HQ. I had few of the best schools and colleges within my orbat for NCC purpose to include "*Sophia Ajmer and Mayo Girls Ajmer*". My predecessor had moved out earlier and the Group Commander was virtually handling my battalion. On my arrival, I found him passing a few decisions against the organizational interest which I resisted. The Group Commander understood my standing and stopped interfering thereafter. I had a vast strength of lady ANOs. My Administrative officer was a lady officer, Capt Pramilla Singh and also had three GCIs (Girl Cadet Instructors). During any conference I would be the lone male member amongst the total strength of 25. I would like to state an extraordinary anecdote of my Camp with the Girls at Udaipur........ One morning, I as Camp Commandant was taking a round of the camp with my Administrative officer, Capt Pramilla. When I approached the visitor's area which was away from the living area of cadets, I could notice one extremely elegant lady draped in white silk sari with golden border and poloroid shades, hiding behind a tent and watching something. I got curious and approached the lady and asked "*Good morning ma'am, can I help you? I find you are very inquisitive of something*". She gathered courage as she could realize me as the Camp Commandant talking to her and replied, "*Colonel, my daughter is your cadet from Mayo Girls Ajmer. I am her mother and have never seen her even picking up a glass of water herself to drink. Today I find her picking up a filled LPG gas Cylinder on her shoulder and carrying it to the kitchen. This is impossible and I am weeping in happiness that you have made my girl a true citizen of this wonderful nation*". My chest was full with pride that I am on the right path. There were few parents of Sofia and Mayo girls Ajmer, who got packed meals for their children attending camps. I was taken aback on hearing from those cadets that, "*We don't need it since we get much better food here in the camp*". My certification was approved by the cadets and didn't need so from the Group commander.

My daughter, Ridhima, had passed her class 12 th (CBSE) with flying colors. She secured 95% marks and was selected for St Stephen's college Delhi as well as IGDTU-B Tech in ECE (Indira Gandhi Delhi Technical University). She opted for IGDTU obviously. Madhav had also got a job with a private bank at Saharanpur. I was a relieved man from such responsibilities troubling me in near future. Ridhima during her winter break planned to visit Udaipur and I was more than happy. She was residing in the Girls college hostel at Kashmiri gate, Delhi. She boarded a Volvo and I received her next early morning at Udaipur. The city of Udaipur apart from alluring travellers with its extensive range of tourists attractions and activities, also presents an equally interest range of destinations to visit in close proximity and can be visited within two to three hours of time are Nathdwara (52 km), Ranakpur (93 km), Kumbhalgarh (102 km), and Mount Abu (165 km). Other popular destinations such as Chittorgarh (117 km), Jodhpur (250 km) are also located quite close and can be reached within 4 hours of journey. She had just about 5 days with me at Udaipur and we had a lot to travel and talk simultaneously.

On day one, I got her to my office and thereafter we had an appointment visit to Taj Lake palace with kind courtesy of my earlier Battalion NCC girl cadet who got a job with this prestigious hotel. She had arranged a VIP boat for us to travel to the Hotel where we were given a traditional welcome as per hotel culture and subsequently we were escorted to view all the galleries and the roof top which was mesmerizing. Also known as Jag Niwas, Lake Palace (Taj Lake Palace) is now a luxury hotel with more than 80 rooms and suites. Lake Palace has been built on the island of Jag Niwas in Lake Pichola, which in turn guarantees breath-taking surroundings. Built between 1743 to 1746 during the rule of Maharana Jagat Singh II, this palace turned hotel, still presents the grandeur of bygone eras. Its white and black marble walls, adorned with semi-precious stones, accompanied by lush green gardens, fountains, pillared terraces, etc. make your visit to this palace a memorable one. In continuation we thought to visit the Udaipur City Palace and Jag Mandir being in close viscinity. On the east bank of Lake Pichola, Udaipur City Palace is a glorious palace which comprises of four magnificent massive palaces and many small palaces. Each presenting a spell-biding architectural beauty with beautiful balconies, canopies and towers. The city palace complex also houses a museum. Whereas Jag mandir is used as summer resort and for hosting parties by the royal family, Jag Mandir was built between 1151 to 1652. Its construction can be attributed to three Maharanas of Sisodia Rajputs from Mewar reign. This palace, located on an island in Lake Pichola, comprises of many beautiful structure that in itself is a popular tourist attractions. Gul Mahal, garden courtyard, Datikhana, Bara patharon ka mahal, Zenana mahal and Kunwar pada ka mahal are few of the buildings inside the complex of Jag Mandir. It has been built in the style of Rajput architecture. It was very strenuous on the very first day and we thought of taking a break next day and just walk down to Fatehsagar lake where I actually lived and spoke about earlier. On reaching one end of the lake Ridhima saw a temple on a hillock and was very inquisitive about it. I told her about the Karni mata temple but she would have to climb a lot to reach it. She agreed and we did the climb chatting. The panoramic view of the complete lake and the city around from the temple was magnificent. Day three was outdoor activity and we visited the famous Rankpur Jain temple. This temple is of 15th-century vintage dedicated to Bhagwan Adinatha and built using white marble in the midst of a forest. The temple name is credited to its design of "chaumukha" (with four faces). The construction of the temple and quadrupled image symbolize the Tirthankara's conquest of the four cardinal directions and hence the cosmos. The temple is one of the largest Jain temples and considered one of the five holiest Jain shrines in India and part of Gorwad Panch Tirth. The architecture and stone carvings of the temple are based on the Ancient Mirpur Jain Temple at Mirpur in Rajasthan. From Ranakpur we moved to Kumbhalgarh fort which is Located 84 kms north of Udaipur in the wilderness, Kumbhalgarh is the second most important citadel after Chittorgarh in the Mewar region. Cradled in the Aravali Ranges the fort was built in the 15th century by King Rana Kumbha. The inaccessibility and hostility of the topography lends a semblance of invincibility to the fort. It served the rulers of Mewar as a refuge in times of strife. It is of immense sentimental significance for the people being the birthplace of Mewar's legendary king Maharana Pratap. The fort is self-contained in all respect to withstand a protracted siege. Its defences could be breached only once by the combined armies of the Mughal and of Amber primarily for scarcity of drinking water. The fort also offers a superb bird's eye view of the surroundings. The fort's massive wall stretches some 36 kms with a width enough to take eight horses abreast and considered the second largest wall after China. Maharana Fateh Singh renovated the fort in the 19th century.

We had lunch and moved ahead to Nathdwara temple. It was difficult to enter the temple without a special pass or had to go through a long queue; therefore one of my Lady ANOs from Nathdwara was available to my help and arranged special passes. Nestled amidst the Aravalli Hills, the charming town of Nathdwara literally translates to "The Gateway of the Lord' (Lord Krishna). It is situated in the heart of Rajasthan, on the banks of river Banas and is a pristine picturesque location. It is also a sacred Hindu site and is flocked by thousands of tourists every year. Nathdwara is also famous for "Pichwai Paintings" which are traditional Rajasthani style paintings and terracotta work. It is considered the hub of traditional handicrafts, arts and artefacts. This town also owes its name to this famous temple given the fact that

Nathdwara literally translates to 'Gateway to Shrinathji'. We were jaded by now and were tempted to bypass all other places and reach Udaipur and hit the bed. However, I boosted her morale to visit "Haldi Ghati" which is en route to Udaipur and a very important battle ground. One of the most bloody and fiercest battles ever fought in the Indian history is the 'Battle of Haldighati'. Haldighati is a magical place, appearing like a canvas painted in dark yellow color. The full wind blowing on the field narrates the bravery and valor of Maharana Pratap of Mewar dynasty. Finally our outdoor visit was fructuous and she returned back with wonderful memories to share with her friends. Day four we started our day visiting "Monsoon palace" which was built in 1884 by the Maharana Sajjan Singh, Monsoon palace was used as monsoon resort. It was also used as hunting lodge by the royals of Mewar Kingdom. Also known as Sajjan Garh Palace, it was constructed on the Bansdara hills and presents a breathtaking view of Fateh Sagar Lake. From here we moved to "Saheliyon-ki-Bari" which is also known as the garden of maidens, Saheliyon-ki-Bari was constructed by the Mewar ruler, Maharana Sangram Singh II. An alluring site as build for the 48 women attendants who have accompanied a princess to Udaipur as a part of her dowry. This garden consisting of lotus pool, fountains, kiosks, marble elephants and a museum is a popular place to visit. Last but not the least we visited "Bagore ki Haveli" which is located at Gangaur Ghat, by the side of Lake Pichola, this magnificent palace was built in 18th century by the Prime minister of Mewar- Amar Chand Badwa. With more than 100 rooms showcasing a rich and rare collection of modern art and costumes, and the exquisite interiors which has been made with glass and mirror work. Apart from places we visited in Udaipur, there are still plentiful such attractive places which could not be visited by Ridhima due to paucity of time and she had her further plans to visit her "Nani" (maternal granny) at Mumbai and departed next morning. It was a grand rendezvous with my lovely daughter Ridhima at Udaipur and I felt elated sharing some wonderful moments with her.

RDC (Republic day camp) involves numerous competitions and is the biggest event in NCC. In fact all training activities of all NCC Directorates culminate at the NCC Republic Day Camp at Cariappa Parade Ground, Delhi Cantt which is held from 01 to 29 Jan every year. 1850 Selected NCC Cadets from 17 directorates attend the Camp. The Camp is inaugurated by the Vice President of India and culminates with Prime Minister's Rally on 28 Jan. During the camp visit of Raksha Mantri, Cabinet Ministers, Chief Minister of Delhi, three Service Chiefs and various State Ministers/VIPs are also organized. During the RDC, various competitions are conducted amongst the 17 NCC Directorates to decide the Champion Directorate for award of Prime Minister's Banner. Competitions are keenly contested in various events such as National Integration Awareness presentation, Drill, Line & Flag Area, Cultural Programs i.e. (group song, group dance & ballet), Best Cadet of Senior Division (Boys) and Senior Wing (Girls) in each Service – Army, Navy & Air Discipline and Best Cadet Boys and Girls each from Junior Wing. Aero modeling and Ship modeling are also conducted during RDC. Before RDC, to prepare for the Directorate's team, all Group headquarters have to face the "IGC" (Inter-Group Competition), after IGC, the selected cadets depart to Delhi to represent their respective states as a directorate team.

The Udaipur Group was never on top as far as IGC was concerned in Rajasthan Directorate. In fact the present Group commander never exhibited much zeal towards this competition and we were last in the directorate for the past 5 years. Just one month prior to the launch of IGC team, I was detailed as the IGC commander for Udaipur group and given barely 20 days to prepare the team for the competition without much of resources and funds. In fact the instructor staff was also inadequate. I had always treasured to accept challenges in life irrespective of any circumstances and here was another chance up my sleeve to give a shift to the image of Udaipur group in the complete directorate. I preferred the location of Bhilwara for training being a non-attractive spot where the cadets would not go wayward like at Udaipur and more so my course mate Col AK Parashar was available as CO of an NCC Battalion there who would greatly come to my assistance. I commenced my journey for IGC trophy and made sure all cadets selected had the eye towards the trophy and prepare. We worked day and night for the next 10 days, be it drill, cultural activities, flag area or line area and best cadet for boys or girls. We created an exhaustive bank of questions and answers. The girls of Mayo and Sophia were utilized for competitions related to oration and intelligence whereas the boys and girls from Govt colleges were used for drill and other activities. Soon we were a team to reckon with and even my friend Arun Parashar made an open statement that *"this year the training and preparation of Udaipur group is reflecting on the faces of the cadets as well the complete staff and undoubtedly the hard work of Col Madhur Goyal would bring kudos"*.

The time arrived and "Jaipur here we come"!!

All of us reached Jaipur as per competition protocol and necessary actions towards the documentation part were completed. My Group commander spoke to me and said, *"Madhur, not to worry about the result, but see if few of our cadets could be selected for RDC at Delhi"*. I was unhappy to hear him say such words at the outset of the competition but least bothering about it we put in our heart to it. When the competition was over and the conference of all team leaders as well as the Deputy Director General of Rajasthan Directorate was held, all eyes were on me with a gleam saying that something has extraordinary has been exhibited by Udaipur Group this time. The results were kept secret for a day but everyone was sure of the result in Udaipur's favour. The day of prize distribution arrived and we started to receive prize after prize in individual category. In no time we had a total of 12 trophies in front of Udaipur Group lined up and finally the announcement of best Group to win IGC trophy for year 2012 was made and "Yours truly" got up straight and upright to march smartly to the DDG Rajasthan and receive the winner's trophy. It was a proud moment for Udaipur but the Group Commander was not present in spite of having come to know of the development. A gamut of our cadets were selected for RDC Delhi out of which seven girl cadets of my battalion were selected and three of them were part of 26 Jan Republic day parade on Rajpath and one girl cadet was selected for "*YEP*" (Youth exchange program) to Singapore.

On return back to Udaipur, I laid a table outside the office of the Group Commander on which all 13 trophies were placed. The group Commander was more than pleased to see the change in Udaipur Group's performance which made the Jaipur Group bow down to its glorious sovereignty on IGC trophy of past decade. Indeed it was an awakening call to all officers, PI Staff and ANOs of Udaipur Group who realized that "It's possible if we want to do it".

Winning the IGC made my tenure very comfortable in coming months and I often made a visit home and ensured all is well there. I also took great interest in paying visits to many schools and colleges to deliver motivation lectures to the students. Towards the end of my tenure the final camp I did was the "*NIC*" (National Integration Camp). I could have moved earlier on my posting but the new Group commander who was a gem of a personality reposed a lot of faith in me and requested the Military Secretary's branch to defer the posting by 15 days.

I would like to share with my readers the beautiful experience of my last NCC camp. Over 600 cadets from all over the country-

Northern states of Punjab and Himachal Pradesh to the Southern tip of Tamil Nadu and from the far corners of North Eastern States to Gujarat in the west participated in the 12-day National Integration Camp organized by the NCC Directorate of Rajasthan at Udaipur. Our camp was designed with the theme "Unity in Diversity" with a dose of rich cross country culture experience. The journey started in mid Dec 2014 and the cadets from all over the county side arrived in the city of Lakes, Udaipur. The day started with roll call in the morning followed by PT then lectures delivered by me and Group Commander on Character building, Personality Development, Career counseling, Leadership qualities. Many competitions such as singing, dancing, Group discussion, Debate, Lecturette and Essay writing between cadets of different NCC directorates of the country were conducted. The cadets were taken for sight-seeing to Lake Pichola, City Palace and Fateh Sagar Lake. Since the cadets were in NCC uniform, as they walked through the streets, the local people looked at them curiously and tiny kids came running to say "hi!" and shook hands and greeted them. It was giving them a feel of some celebrity. In fact during their visit to a "Mall", the girl cadets were being addressed as ma'am by the showroom staff and they were taking pride hearing it.

On the last day of the camp *"Bada Khana"* (variety of dishes) was arranged. After summing up the event, few cadets sung *"Chalthe chalthe meri ye geet yaad rakhna, kabhi alvida naa kehnaa..."* It was a happy ending to the camp which went successful as planned. There was a display of fireworks and all cadets regardless of culture, religion or region they came from were holding hands together and screaming with joy at the site of beautiful light patterns in the dark sky. I saw a Mini India or *"Chota Bharat"* in a very short span. It was a sad Good Bye moment!!

I loved my tenure at NCC Udaipur and was all packed in my Ford Ikon to travel back 950 Kms where I started from, Saharanpur. My next posting was out but this time the most challenging of all previous ones. I was posted on a coveted appointment of "Administrative Commandant" of Nahan Military Station. Nahan is like a home station for all Special Forces personal of Army Para Commandos. I was to report by early Feb 2015 and by then would be home with my Mom, Shikha and Madhav.

Chapter XVI

The Final Punch with Special Forces

"A true leader has the confidence to stand alone, the courage to make tough decisions, and the compassion to listen to the needs of others. He does not set out to be a leader, but becomes one by the equality of his actions and the integrity of his intent".

– Douglas MacArthur

I was joining Nahan in winters. Another place of wind, chill and thrill!!

It was my first drive from Saharanpur to Nahan in mid Jan 2015, not far but just 98 Km away which took me exactly 1 hr and 45 mins to reach. The last stretch of 19 Km was a hilly terrain and bit curvy and time consuming. This would be my all weekend routine from Nahan to Saharanpur and back. Reaching Nahan, I found the cantonment area was a separate entity altogether on a different hillock and away from the hustle bustle of the town. I drove down straight to the Station Headquarters location and reported my arrival.

Nahan is a township as well as the headquarters of Sirmaur District in Himachal Pradesh. It was the capital of the former Sirmur princely state and is located at an average elevation of 3000 ft. Nahan is situated on a hill top overlooking the green Shivalik Hills. Traditionally, saints and princes are linked with the origin of Nahan.

The city was founded in 1621 by Raja Karam Prakash. Another version recalls a saint who lived with a companion named Nahar on the site where the Nahan palace now stands. "Nahar" means 'don't kill' and the town probably takes its name from an incident when a king was trying to kill a lion and the saint said Nahar that is 'do not kill it'. The name of the saint was Baba Banwari Das, so it was named Nahar and later called Nahan, which is distortion of Nahar. Nahan is a used as a base for visits to the surrounding areas such as Renuka Lake, Paonta Sahib, Trilokpur and the Suketi Fossil Park. It is watered by a man-made lake and has several temples and gardens. Nahan has got the crown to organize the second Municipal Corporation in India, after Kolkata. Underground sewerage system in this town is unbeatable and hence it bears the title to be a neat and clean town. Well planned streets make all the long distances calm and traffic-free. The narrow fields are used by the pedestrians to move fast on foot to avoid traffic. The gentle level walks of Villa Round and Hospital Round (Chakkar Ke Sadak) are evocative of the city's past. The hub of Nahan's activities is Chaugan. The Mall Road is one of the favourite places of the youngsters after the college campus to walk along, especially in evening.

The Officer who was to hand over to me was on one month's leave and had got his posting delayed by two months hence, I was in waiting as an "Additional Officer" to take over charge on relinquishment of his appointment. This period helped me a great deal to understand the nuances of Nahan military station and its shortcomings specially. I made good liaison with the district authorities and various officers in station. We also had an Army public school up to 12th standard and I was an important member in its management committee. The other units in station were a Battalion of Special Forces (elite commandoes), Special forces training school which was a training establishment, Station Headquarters which was my establishment and elements of Garrison engineer. I occupied a Single officer's accommodation in the SFTS officer's mess which was well equipped to my needs.

The SFTS (Special Forces Training School is responsible to churn out the elite Special Forces of the Indian Army. The Commandant of the school is also designated as the Station Commander and my immediate superior. The School owes its origin to a humble beginning on 01 Apr 1993 where it was established as a Special Forces Training Wing (SFTW) to impart training to the then 3 Para Commando battalions. The aim of raising this School was to provide unique and specialist training which was not available in any other training institution. The raising of this school gave a boost to up gradation of the parachute commando battalions to Special Forces which were capable of conducting a wide variety of strategic and operational tasks, both overt and covert, in war and low intensity conflict situations. The essence of training at SFTS is 'Walk the Talk' where absolute professional competence is built through a practical on ground training. The students are trained to be confident and develop a strong winning attitude for carrying out special operations in the entire spectrum of contemporary warfare. SFTS is a Centre of Excellence (COE) for Special Forces' Training and is also nominated as Nodal Agency for training with Special Forces of Friendly Foreign Countries (FFC). The Indian Army conducts joint Special Forces exercises and training with the special forces of countries such as the United Kingdom, Seychelles, United States, Sri Lanka, Russia, France, Bangladesh and Thailand at this school. The motto of the School is "*Sauryam Daksham Yuddhe*" which means "Courage and Competence in War".

This was the first instance in my career of past 30 years then that I ever served with Special Forces personnel or its units/establishments. I found their officers to be with behavioral and attitudinal difference as compared to the rest of the armed forces personnel. It was subsequently that I realized "His aptitude is his attitude". It takes a special desire to seek out the challenge and it takes special ability to perform the mission. The training is intensive and comprehensive. It takes mental toughness to complete the training and dedication to maintain the proficiency needed to do the many tasks required. Physical fitness is only a part of the package. Weapons proficiency, language skills, tactics, logistics, and the ability to train and lead other troops are what make Special Forces soldiers special. They are skilled in basically everything they do, whether sniping or cutting open a can of beans. But what really separates them from the grunts is their mental determination. Special Forces training aims to separate the mentally weak from the mentally strong, and then build up the ones who make it.

Finally the day arrived in Mar 2015 when I took over as Administrative Commandant and got fully absorbed in my daily routine. During my interim period at Nahan I had very well gathered the major handicap in station matters was related to Defence Land issues. When the princely State Forces of Sirmur integrated with the constitution of India, Indian Army took over a total of 556 acres of land in 1954 out of which mutation of only 459 acres was done in 1979 by the revenue department resulting in a deficiency of 96 acres (given to villagers under Land Reforms and Tenancy Act 1972). Out of 459 acres of land mutated in favor of Army, 27.15 acres was under encroachment/In Possession by land dons. This land issue became my focus thereafter and I took it as a challenge to resolve it out before I finally leave Nahan. I read all possible documents of old vintage and kept flagging them for future reference. Meanwhile the honorable High Court at Shimla passed a "suo motto" verdict that all barriers within the military station to be removed and the road to be free for move of locals. This resulted in grave danger for the entire campus as such. I was told by the Station Commander to visit Shimla earliest and discuss the issue with the ASGI (Assistant Solicitor General of India) and if possible arrange a meeting with the honorable Chief

Justice to convey our point of view before the counter affidavit reply is read in the court on the suo motto verdict. I met the ASGI and conveyed my point of view which was accepted by him to fight it out in the next hearing. However, he also recommended if I get a chance to meet the honorable CJ for which I was ready. He somehow managed to arrange a short meeting in CJ's personal chamber. With due respects I conveyed the unforeseen danger within the porous cantonment of Nahan after the verdict to the CJ. I also conveyed the likelihood of miscreants aiming to target certain soft targets since the Special Forces are generally out on operations or training. I quoted the recent episode of Pathankot air force station. The honorable CJ was hearing very keenly and understood the importance of safe guarding the military station. I returned back to Nahan the same evening and to the surprise of all and sundry, the suo motto order was reversed to status quo. It brought cheers to the entire military fraternity of Nahan military station as well as my superior HQs at Ambala and Chandimandir.

My Disaster Management course at College of Military Engineering, Pune was enlisted and I was to proceed in July 2015. It was a nice break though from the busy schedule at Nahan. Apart from my course schedule, I had plenty of friends and course mates there. It was a big fun mixing studies and pleasure. It was a great learning on Chemical, Radiological, Biological and Nuclear warfare. We also had an attachment with AFMC Pune to learn about dealing with emergencies during various medical issues. There were a few 20 Jat officers at Pune and we had a get together at Col VV Chandran's place. Whereas our course mates got together at the CME officers institute. I even recollect, my late wife Reena's mom and brother and his wife drove down all the way from Mumbai to meet me. We had lunch together too. I recollect once at the boating club of CME, I was posing for a pic where as suddenly I found myself losing the balance and the boat toppled and I was deep down in the CME Lake with boat over me as a boat cap on my head. I had always been a good swimmer so I extricated myself well in time but it was a big embarrassing moment in front of my course mates and the ladies too. Returning back to Nahan I was now firm on clearing encroachments from my defence land. The district administration was not too eager to unnecessarily face wrath of locals when the state elections were nearing. Irrespective I got the clearance of the Station Commander and we initially cleared three of them which were very open and obvious ones. The Station received kudos for it and my work was highly appreciated by the Army Commander.

I was to superannuate on 31 Oct 2017. This entails that my documentation in various phases as prescribed by the Army HQs should start reaching them from one year backwards. I got on to the list of documents and earmarked my head clerk to prepare and dispatch as per correct timelines. I was given an option of additional four years of service after the age of 54 but I declined and firmed on settling down at Saharanpur with my lovely family who were awaiting my arrival. Meanwhile I learnt that my parent unit "20 Jat" which was at Alwar (Rajasthan) was moving out of station and would be passing by Ambala. I ensured that they make a night halt at Ambala and made all possible arrangements for the entire Battalion to stay in comfort. I arranged guest rooms for all officers who were single as well as with their ladies and children. We had a nice get together in the Sub Area mess followed with dinner where many more 20 Jat veterans and serving officers residing at Chandigarh and around also joined in. It was indeed memorable to be with your Battalion where you were born as an officer. The fraternity of 20 Jat conveyed their gratitude on this gesture.

My daughter Ridhima and her friend Saumya (studying together and roommates) had arrived at Saharanpur on a break and wanted to visit Nahan for a few days. The coming weekend during my trip to Saharanpur, I picked them up to Nahan in my car and had also arranged a guest room for them. We had a nice outdoor visit to Renuka Lake and a special isolated resort on the mountain top. They loved the trip. I arranged their visit to the Special Forces unit where they got a chance to witness all latest Special Forces weapons and the training area. They would hold the guns and feel like commandoes themselves. They saw the snake pit and the ten meter Lido jump too. They enjoyed their meals at the SFTs officers mess. I left them on completion of their visit at Ambala Railway station since they had their booking back to Delhi from there.

It was May 2016; there was a change of Command in SFTS which also meant a change of Station Commander for the Station. The new Commander was much more a dare devil than the previous one and more gelling with me too. He had a similar thought process on station matters as I had and we both played merry hell with the land mafia of Nahan and ensured that the Army gets back its full complement of encroached land back from the miscreants. During yr 2016 a total of four encroachment cases were removed and approx 36 bighas of Defence land recovered and fresh notice to eight encroachment cases was issued under PPE Act 1971 involving a total of approx 28 bighas of Defence Land. The Army Commander Western Command made an open statement during one of the briefings at Sub Area Ambala that, "It's only the Administrative Commandant at Nahan who is getting our defence land back to Army unlike others who are sitting quiet". I was recommended for GOC-In-C Western Command Commendation Card subsequently. I had a big portfolio, however, I have only stressed on the major issue of Land matters which needed to be addressed in correct earnest.

I was completing 32 years of commissioned service with three rows of medals on my chest and a special Gallantry award. Now I thought it's enough of serving "motherland", now is the time to serve "my mother" instead. My focus shifted a bit and was more towards completing my retirement documentation thereon. The COAS (Chief of Army Staff) had started a very nice procedure of organizing a ROS (Retiring officer's seminar) at Delhi wherein all officers retiring in that particular month would be invited and given a warm send off by the Chief. It was a two day event involving documentation, meeting the respective Generals, clearing all doubts pertaining to your pay and Pension there on and finally meet the Chief who physically hands over the famous folder with all our original documents to us. My time also arrived and I took Shikha along with me to Delhi. We had our guest room allotted in the Infantry Mess. It was a memorable stay and the event was managed with grandeur. We also got an evening off to dine with my daughter, Ridhima at DSOI Dhaula kuan since she was still pursuing her engineering at Delhi. On my return I dropped Shikha back at Saharanpur and proceeded to Nahan. I always made a point to take strawberries to Saharanpur on all my weekends.

My reliever's posting was out and I was waiting for him to reach Nahan as early as possible. The handing taking over of the appointment of Administrative Commandant was formalized on his arrival and I was a free man although I still had two days to leave Nahan. I tried to give my best brief to the new incumbent on Land issues of Nahan which was the hot topic and Nahan Station headquarters had gained lot of ascendency because of this. In fact all other officers at various stations would invariably call us to know the tact we were following to clear encroachments. My dining out was earmarked a night prior to my move out permanently from Nahan which was a memorable one. The speech made by the Station Commander still echoes my ear drums who spoke very high words in my favor. I was to leave first with lot of hugging with all officers present at the party. Next morning I was given a fantastic send off by pulling my car with a rope as a traditional procedure when an officer proceeds on retirement.

I was on my way home finally after my strong 32 years of commissioned service.

Here I come………. Saharanpur……!!!

"The veterans of our military services have put their lives on the line to protect the freedoms that we enjoy. They have dedicated their lives to their country and deserve to be recognized for their commitment".

– Judd Gregg

Chapter XVII

The Twilight Years: Family Harmony

It was a wonderful sunny morning of 01 Nov 2017 and I was driving back to Saharanpur in my Ford Ikon with all its pockets full. The gentle and cool breeze indicating the advent of winters was very comforting and I kept all the windows open and continued driving like a man who just got his liberty. The entire route, I had a smile on my face which I could not view but felt it so dearly for the first time. Those lovely thoughts of now not waking up early in the morning, not shaving daily to the office and staying home in my Bermuda's was indeed giving me an adrenaline rush. I reached home with a basket full of Strawberries once again and my wife Shikha, mom and son Madhav welcomed the Soldier home for the first time after shedding his Olive Green's.

Retirement constitutes a major transition in soldier's life. It ushers in a new stage in the life's course, which requires restructuring of daily routine and social contacts. It is not like jumping off a diving board, it's a process and it takes time. There's a lot of work people do to prepare for it. The questions most people think about before retirement are *"How much money will I need?"* and *"Am I saving enough?"* But while financial security is certainly critical, people need to amass a stockpile of their emotional reserves as well for a successful retirement. Some retirees ease smoothly into retirement, spending more time with hobbies or family and friends. However, there are always potential wild cards that can shape retirement in unexpected and undesirable directions such as anxiety, depression and debilitating feelings of loss.

I was very clear in my mind that I wanted the sleeping author, sleeping poet and the sleeping stock marketer inside me to wake up from a deep slumber and rejuvenate. I already had a prefix and a suffix to my name endorsed by the Armed forces for life; however, I wished to create another entity for myself in my second innings which would be special enough. I started interacting with all my relations and lost friends even more and made a good social circle to gel with. I took up membership of an elite club at Saharanpur which would cater for my weekends along with my family. I started to give much more time for household chores to assist my wife and mom thereby bringing back smiles on their face. I gave a facelift to my existing small house and made it more appropriate for visitors to visit. In fact I experienced umpteen course mates who visited me and still doing so. My Facebook and Whatsapp friend circle and groups expanded beyond imagination and enjoyed chatting with friends often and on. The first major wish that I fulfilled on my homecoming was to visit "*Shri Mahaveer ji*" our pilgrimage site for Jains. Shri Mahaveer Ji temple is in Karauli district in Rajasthan, earlier known as Chandanpur, this small village became famous as a Jain religious site after an ancient idol of "Lord Mahaveer" was excavated from its soil several hundred years ago. It was then renamed as "Shri Mahaveer Ji". This idol was excavated over 200 years ago from the same spot, after which the temple was constructed. Thousands of worshipers flock from across India to catch a glimpse of this famous statue. Ridhima had also graduated in her engineering and was placed with "Ericson Global" at Delhi. She joined us at Saharanpur and all five of us in Ford Ikon proceeded on a long drive ahead to the holy place of Jainism. Visiting Mahaveer ji also gave me an opportunity of making a night halt either way at my sister's place in Noida. Meeting my sister, Ruby for first time after retirement was a blessing too. I can say with conviction that this was the first festival of Diwali followed by the New year's that was celebrated with my complete heart and soul and with my family without any hindrance that I need to get up early next morning to drive back to work.

Come 2018, brought cheers to the money markets and subsequently the US – China strained trade relations were dampening the hopes of big brokers. There was a big fall in the stock markets globally and many small industries and financial companies witnessed lock outs. I was given great news by Ridhima who was selected for her "Masters in Management course" at "Singapore Management University". She was granted scholarship too. Her course would commence from early Jan 2019 and therefore she booked her tickets for end Dec 2018 since her bestie friend "Saumya" was already doing her "Masters in Computer Science" from "National University of Singapore" and they wanted to witness the famous New Year's fireworks together at Marina Bay.

Majority of our 77' regular course mates of IMA Dec 1985 batch had already retired and had come up with an idea of having an extravagant get together at Goa during Oct-Nov 2018. Col Austin Collaco my commando buddy and a dear friend being a local from Goa and also employed after retirement with the Govt of Goa took on the responsibility of arranging this big bash. He was assisted by Col Shiva Waradkar another course mate friend of mine posted on re-employment at Goa. We were almost 50 couples who gave our assent to visit and started preparing for the event. I along with Shikha got our flights booked ex Delhi to Goa and Back. Ridhima had come over to Saharanpur on leave and was assisting Mom since Madhav was to go to office and leaving mom alone was not a wise idea. Finally, the day arrived and me and Shikha departed by Shatabdi express to Delhi and checked into our earlier booked room at DSOI Dhaukla Kuan for the night since next morning was our flight. I met my dear pal and course mate, Col Nitin Chandra, at DSOI who was also travelling with his wife for the same event. Next morning we mustered up at the airport and found two more of our course mate couples for the same destination. Reaching the hotel at Goa and meeting the *"band of brothers"* was indeed an emotional one. We met like we never grew beyond *"gentlemen cadets"* after "Indian Military Academy". Our lady wives were awestruck to witness such closeness and camaraderie still existing amongst us. The arrangements were stupendous and the *"Goan duo"* had really worked hard to arrange it all for us. We had a dinner on cruise, a massive dinner at "The Taj", a Goan cuisine luncheon and sumptuous breakfast all days of stay. Apart from centrally arranged activities we also visited variety of beaches and other tourist attractions at Goa. Three days were not enough to satiate us but more than enough to tire us out. We finally returned with attractive return gifts arranged by the organizers to keep these sweet memories of Goa forever. We also took a vow to meet every year at a pre decided place.

On my return, I learnt about the wedding of Rahul, son of Col Rishi Moitra of 20 Jat. The wedding venue was at Kolkatta and I was keen to attend for two main reasons, firstly, I could not attend his daughter, Ritu's wedding earlier and secondly, I had never witnessed a Bengali wedding before. This time I had to leave alone since Ridhima was at Delhi and was preparing for her departure to Singapore by the end of the year. I recalled my last visit to Kolkata during return from honeymoon from Andamans in 1990, now it was early Dec 2018. It was 4.45 pm and my flight was about to land. The sun sets much earlier in the east and hides by 5.00 pm making it pitch dark. I witnessed the sun disappearing, shrouding the entire city in its bluish afterglow. I was well received and driven to the hotel where all the other guests were accommodated, en route I could sense the warm smell of mustard and fish permeating my sinus reminiscing the land to which I always had a strong bond attached from my youngster days. On reaching the hotel I converged on to my battalion officers and families with a quick session of *"pappi jhappi"* (hugs and kisses) and simultaneously all of us swamping Rishi Moitra. It was like a yuletide. The love, one has for something isn't measured by how one feels while parting with it, but while uniting after parting. The words couldn't have been truer to elucidate the feeling of homecoming at Kolkatta. The groom's father called me, *"Dusht"* you are always late!! Its baraat time and you have to change. To be on his dearer side, I dressed for the occasion akin to his choice in *"pyjama kurta"* and not "dhoti" for obvious reasons. The Bengali rituals of baraat commenced with the groom's mom welcoming son Rahul by crowning him with groom's headgear and thereafter we all left for the marriage venue. Rituals true to the occasion maintaining the sanctity of bengali culture were performed and I along with my present mates cherished each activity with great enthusiasm. Suddenly, I witnessed a much known figure in the gathering and I shouted.....Joy...!! He rightly looked towards the direction of the sound and met my eyes like a true infantry soldier. Col Joydeep Dey, my course mate at IMA having spent those fun-filled (pun intended) days of training for 18 months together. Our reunion post three decades was bit embarrassing and not befitting the occasion but welcomed by multitude being a majority gathering of army guys. We chatted and exchanged our miseries for an hour followed by the sumptuous wedding meal, although difficult for me to choose from the dishes being a pure veggie. The entire ceremony clicked just about three hours and we returned home with a sweet lil' bengali doll as a bride for dear Rahul. Overall, the simplicity of a bengali wedding erased all my faulty images of a big fat north Indian wedding. I retired to my hotel room, lay on the bed and heaved the sigh I had been holding for a while. The much awaited evening arrived and we all ganged up at the banquet hall for the gala reception of the blessed lovely married couple. Looking at Rahul, brought his childhood image in front of my eyes. As the evening passed, the confidence got more spirited and the discussions took rapid U turns. The gala photo sessions followed by multi cuisine dinner spread was memorable. We all had to catch an early flight next day back to our places of residence/offices.

My Dec month was packed with action and the moment I returned from Kolkatta got busy in packing up of Ridhima to Singapore. She was seen off by her *"Amma"* (as she calls my mom), Shikha and Madhav. I drove her down to Noida where she stayed for the day with my sister Ruby and later I and Udit saw her off to the airport by midnight. I spent the the night at my sister's place and next morning on receiving conformation of Ridhima's safe arrival at Singapore, I returned back to Saharanpur. Year 2019 arrived but this time less action packed and more of handling local domestic issues. Our course had planned the next social get together at Bhimtal close to Nainital. Although the gathering was not too large this time but we had a great time together. It was much easier to identify everyone and especially so the ladies knew each other by now. My sister Ruby and Sudhir Jijaji had come over to Saharanpur for the period of our absence due to which I and Shikha could manage to move for the event.

It has been almost three years now that I shed my Olive greens……. I do miss the icy himalayan wind, chill and thrill, hot lazy sun of the deserts, wild adventures of the jungles and the waves dispensing its anger on the ocean floor. Now I live in the hustle-bustle of city life, Saharanpur that seems to be caring now. I don't feel like a stranger anymore!! The month of Jan 2020 was an ecstatic month for money markets. In spite of economy in doldrums still we saw the benchmark indices at all-time high. Made good money on intraday trade. Come Feb and we saw another big event of Mr Trump visiting India. Side by side we kept on hearing of the deadly Covid 19 virus spreading its wrath all over Wuhan state of China like wild fire and resulting in numerous casualties. We still kept up the tempo of *"NaMoste Trump"* and all is well that ends well. The month of March rang the bells all over the nation followed by burning of *"divas"* and banging *"thalis"* but the damn virus wouldn't budge. It had established its platform and tactically sighting its bunkers for an unostentatious attack. As per the Disaster management policy, orange alert was announced and the *"lockdown"* commenced. We had heard of *"black outs"* during war scenario but this lockdown occurred for the first time in my life so far.

When the lockdown started, I was ecstatic, the sun was shining. I was happy, and confident I would be OK. After all, how hard could staying at home possibly be? The first few days passed with web series on Netflix and Amazon Prime. After a while, the reality of the situation started to sink in. The novelty of being at home wore off and I started to struggle. I had nightmares most nights, and struggled to sleep. It was as if I was stuck, trapped in my house and in my own head. I didn't know how to cope. However, over time, I found ways to deal with the pressure. I realized that lockdown gave me more time to the things I loved, hobbies that had been previously swamped by routine army duty. I started baking, drawing and writing again, and felt free for the first time in months. I had forgotten how good it felt to be creative. I started spending more time with my family. I hadn't realized how much I had missed them. Almost a month later, I feel so much better. I understand how difficult this must be, but it's important to remember that none of us is alone. No matter how scared, or trapped, or alone you feel, things can only get better. Take time to revisit the things you love, and remember that all of this will eventually pass. All we can do right now is stay at home, look after ourselves and our loved ones, and look forward to a better future. The virus travelled without restraint across the planet, affecting millions. It showed us that not everyone had the same access to treatment and protection, that the world we'd built was not a fair one. But it also laid out the initial sparks of real change, teaching us how interconnected we all are and how fragile the balance between humanity and nature is.

One of the most important responses to COVID-19 was getting people to stay at home. When people stayed home, there was less travel. Less travel meant less air pollution. Very quickly, our air and water became cleaner. Nature reclaimed its space and shape. We stopped seeing grey skies above great cities because of pollution. Now, I'm not saying a pandemic was the solution we wanted to our complex environmental challenges. Certainly not, but coronavirus did serve as a grim reminder about how humans have taken over the Earth, exploited resources and habitats of every other living species. It reminded us that not only do humans not own the planet, that we share it equally with other living beings. Our life is about respectful cohabitation, and unless we learned to coexist, nature would find extreme ways to reclaim its space. Surely, we were extraordinarily resilient in overcoming the crisis and reshaping the world for the better. I take this sad opportunity to add on with deep sorrow that two of my best friends succumbed into the cruel hands of **"*Covid 19*"** in September/October 2020, namely **"*Col Sirang Dhamankar*"** (my Army course mate) and **"*Mr Kapil Kohli*"** (My school Classmate). I on behalf of the brethren of IMA 77' regular course and Naval public school 1979 class 10th batch, convey our deepest condolences to their families and pray to God Almighty to bless and grant "Sadgati"(salvation) to the noble souls.

Lost in thoughts, sipping green tea, I didn't even realize how the morning became noon and I was lost in the world of emotions watching people with face masks, gloves and ambulance vehicles ringing past. In these formative years, we will make some important choices, and no matter what choice we make, I hope we make it our life's work to apply our brilliant minds and tender hearts towards solving some of our world's toughest challenges.

I have reached the culmination of my book here narrating 37 years of my memoirs commencing from joining the Indian Military Academy at Dehradun to completion of three years after retirement. Before parting dear readers, I would like to state that I have always been a strong follower of word "**Perseverance**". Rightly said by **Albert Einstein**, "***It's not that I'm so smart, it's just that I stay with problems longer***". Follow it and you will see the change in you. I sign off paying "*an ode to my retirement*" a poem I wrote after finally reaching home after retirement from active army service ....

An Ode to my Retirement

My wayfare in olive green commenced more than three decades ago,

Bewedded the Indian Military Academy with gentleman cadets I later came to know.

Trained hard, setting high standards for self,

Displaying honor, pride, dignity and nothing else.

Sought a divine route and a heart to do HIS will,

Soldiering became a passion with all my skills.

Umpteen operations favorably completed,

Countless tasks efficiently concluded.

Endless nights spent under gunfire, inclement weather and inhospitable terrain,

Those unforgettable experiences bring chill to my purple vein.

Reysed far and wide,

Purpose awaited me on every side.

Find adventure in all....is that what suits me?

Or write an Ode to my OG's by the shade of a tree.

But now is the time to put myself first,

Relax, enjoy, live life and fulfill all my thirst.

But never forget as I go along, honestly right from the start,

Thrilling moments I shared for many years, left an imprint... right here...

On my Heart!!

And in the quiet of my heart,

I hear my God softly say.......

"My dear ardent enthusiastic admirer,

I am proud of you this day!!!!!!!

— Col Madhur Goyal, SM (retd)

Made in the USA
Monee, IL
11 April 2021